MW01640189

THE FAMILY
VILLAGE

LEE

LEE

THE FAMILY

CHAPTER 1

ALL FUN AND GAMES

On a warm spring evening, Tineshia, 17yrs old, 5'9 175lbs with an almond complexion and curly freshly braided ombre hair, along with Zahra, 18 yrs old, 5'7 150lbs expresso skin color with straight jet black hair, have been drinking at a house party towards the end of spring break. Although they have had a few drinks they are nowhere near drunk. They are in a community where every house has a well manicured lawn, three car garage and fenced in backyard. It is 1:48 am and Zahra is spending the weekend at Tineshia's parents' house, which is a 25-minute drive away from the party.

While waiting outside for their LYFT, which falsely said it was there, Tineshia is playing music from her phone and Zahra is dancing. A nosey neighbor, who has designated herself the head of a non-existent Neighborhood Watch, notices the two young ladies standing outside and calls the police. A Lyft pulls up one house down and across the street from them. Three teenage white women, Haley 15 years old and 5'4, Brittany 16 years old and 5'3, and Jennifer 16 years old and 5'3, get out of the car.

While walking down the street, Jennifer is very loud and screaming song lyrics. Haley is trying to quiet her down, while Brittany is mouthing along and dancing. Brittany and Jennifer are visibly drunk. They were supposed to have been home no later than 1:00 a.m. As they walk towards Haley's parents' house, three houses down, Jennifer notices Zahra dancing. Jennifer stops singing and approaches the two black girls. She crosses the street, stumbling, and calls out towards the young girls.

"Hey, I know that song. I know that dance, but you're doing it wrong." says Jennifer badly slurred.

Haley again tries to get Jennifer to quiet down. "Jenn, shhh, my mom is going to hear us." Jennifer, now standing in front of the two black women, starts trying to do the dance Zahra was just doing. "Hey, Britt, lets show them how it's supposed to go." Now Brittany and Jennifer both are dancing and singing along to the song still playing from Tineshia's phone.

Zahra and Tineshia look at each other, trying their best to not laugh, but after a few seconds. Zahra can't hold it any longer and burst out laughing, followed by Tineshia. Jennifer takes offense to them laughing and stops dancing, but Brittany continues to carry right along.

"What the hell is so funny?" Jennifer asks. Tineshia and Zahra, still laughing, wave their hands and can barely get a word out, saying nothing in between laughs.

No longer does Jennifer just find this offensive, she is now angry and takes a few steps toward the black women. Haley is right behind her. Tineshia notices Jennifer's advance and change in demeanor and taps Zahra to get her to focus and realize the mood has shifted. Zahra looks up notices Brittany still dancing and singing, and starts laughing harder. Jennifer looks behind her and notices Brittany and yells, "Britt, stop dancing. These girls think we're a joke."

Haley says. "Did you two just move around here or something? I haven't seen you before."

"No we were just visiting some friends," says Tineshia.

"Come on Haley," interrupts Jennifer. Just look at them. You know they couldn't live over here."

Zahra now no longer laughing. "What the *fuck* that supposed to mean?"

Jennifer has a smirk on her face, knowing she struck a nerve. "Well, I mean, look around. Not many single baby mothers can afford to live over here... you know, depending on child support checks and all."

Zahra, just lost her father to heart disease only three months ago. She has skipped right past angry and is totally enraged. "*Bitch!* You don't know me." She starts to go after Jennifer. Tineshia, knowing what her best friend has been dealing with, quickly gets in front of Zahra and holds her back.

Jennifer, seeing the pain she has inflicted now, has a look of accomplishment on her face. Haley, also noticing the pain evident on Zahra's face, taps Jennifer on the arm and gives a nod towards her parents' house. "Come on, ladies, let's go in the house before whatever drug dealer they're probably waiting for pulls up."

"Keep it 100." Jennifer says as she smiles and starts walking towards Haley's parents' house. While Tineshia is holding Zahra back. Haley, walking behind Jennifer, starts laughing as she passes.

Zahra livid and enraged, is screaming now. "Fuck you! I will beat all three of you. Fucking let me go."

Brittany, totally oblivious to what has been going on, and still zoned out. She keeps two step dancing, stumbles and steps on Tineshia's foot as she passes. Tineshia flinches and momentarily loses control of Zahra.

Zahra breaks free, grabs Brittany by the hair, spinning her around, and hits her in the face, dropping her to the ground. Jennifer and Haley, hearing their friend hit the ground, turn around and see her on the ground. A look of shock and fear comes over Haley's face, while Jennifer wears an almost sinister grin.

"Oh, y'all thought it was a game, huh?" Zahra yells with her hands up. She starts to go after the focus of her rage... Jennifer.

Brittany is on the ground crying and bleeding with her purse wide open and all her belongings spread over the street, as Zahra starts after Jennifer.

Haley swings at Zahra out of fear. Zahra senses the punch and dodges it. She turns towards Haley, shocked. "*Bitch*!" Zahra yells.

Jennifer notices the distraction and takes advantage. Jennifer grabs Zahra by the hair and starts swinging wildly.

Tineshia, still shaking off the pain of being stepped on, sees Haley swing at her friend and without a second thought goes after her. Tineshia grabs her and slings her to the ground. Her purse flies off her arm, landing five feet away. Tineshia jumps on her and starts to swing, but before she can throw her punch, the nosey neighbor comes running out of her house, yelling.

Tineshia notices the neighbor coming towards them, then looks down the street. She sees the lights of a police car. In the excitement neither Tineshia nor Zahra heard the sirens. She gets off Haley and hits Jennifer in the ribs, causing her to release her grip on Zahra's hair. Tineshia tries to pull Zahra away to run, but Zahra, still enraged, pulls away and hits Jennifer in the face knocking her to the ground.

Tineshia turns towards her friend and yells, "Z! *Cops*!" Zahra looks up and notices the police car getting closer.

"*Shit*!"

She and Tineshia take off running. The police cruiser stops, and two officers one black woman and one white man hop out.

The nosey neighbor now, standing over Haley, Brittney, and Jennifer, is yelling, "There they go... over there. They're trying to get away."

Tineshia and Zahra both take off back towards the side gate of the house they were previously partying at. Zahra clears the fence with no issue, but Tineshia, still feeling the effects of being stepped on, stumbles. Zahra stops running and looks back at her friend.

"Keep going," Tineshia yells. As she tries to get up and prepare to jump the fence. But before she can, the male officer tackles her and begins to arrest her. *"Run!"* Tineshia yells again. Zahra takes off running.

The male officer nods to the lady officer. "The other

one trying to get away...catch her." Then he starts reading Tineshia her rights and putting the cuffs on her.

Zahra runs around the side of the house towards the back. She runs into Derek, a seventeen-year-old white boy with blond hair, dressed in a tee-shirt and skinny jeans and Jordan shoes with two fake chains on his neck. Derek had been trying to get Zahra's attention all night. He is standing outside by himself smoking weed.

"Hey, little mama. I knew I was going to see you again. It has to be a sign, you really should get to know me, why don't you give me those digits."

Zahra, trying to think quickly, "Sure. Let's go inside so I can get my phone and get yours too."

Derek, a little shocked, overly happy, and a little high, grabs her hand, and walks her in the house. By the time the black officer has made it to the back, Zahra and Derek have already gone inside and locked the door.

The officer comes back around front and informs her partner that she has lost the suspect but heard music and voices coming from the house and believes the suspect may have slipped inside. Her partner, already having placed Tineshia in the back of the cruiser, joins her and the officers ring the doorbell. Derek and Zahra are in the living room. Zahra is very nervous, knowing who is at the door. When another of the teens opens the door, and before the police can say anything,

"*Police*!" Zahra yells.

All the kids become nervous, since most have been smoking, doing drugs, and almost everyone was underage and drinking, they stampede towards the back door trying to get away. Once outside, "This shit crazy. Do you have a car? Don't you want to make sure I get home safely?" Zahra asks flirtatiously.

In the mad dash of kids running and since neither officer got a clear look at Zahra, she has no problem slipping away in the crowd.

CHAPTER 2

HARSH REALITY

Two additional police cruisers arrive to assist. I'll stay and finish collecting statements. Go ahead and get her back to our house. says the male officer.

The lady officer gets in the car with Tineshia and starts driving to the precinct. "What the hell was all that about?" she asks. Tineshia stays quiet. "Do you live in the neighborhood, or were you just at the party?" Tineshia stares out the car window and remains silent. "That's crazy your friend just left you like that. She didn't stop to help you or anything. She just going to let you take the whole rap?"

"Rap?" responds Tineshia.

"Yeah. You think those girls not going to press charges? Not to mention we have an overly enthusiastic witness."

Tineshia shakes her head. "I'm under eighteen and I want to talk to my parents, and I want a lawyer"

"Oh, I thought you were different," says the officer, "but you're a natural at this. You been here before huh?"

Tineshia continues to look out the window and stays silent.

"It's cool after we get your prints, we will get your full rap sheet. I was just trying to help you baby girl, but you don't want my help, that's fine. You can stay silent. I was just trying to assist you sister to sister, but you want to play the ghetto girl role by, all means go right ahead."

Tineshia leans back and looks at the officer with disgust, "*Sister to sister, huh*? Let's be clear, you ain't my sister. You blue. True blue, the way you sounding. Ghetto girl? Nah. I'm just not that dumb." Tineshia cocks her head to the side. "Baby girl, you not going to run game on me. Now, you have my ID and know my name is not 'baby girl' and you know my age. I also have told you I'm underage and I want to speak to parents or a lawyer. So, at this point are you even allowed to speak to me anymore? Anything I would say now would be inadmissible, right? Or are you so blue you done turned your body cam off already and trying to get an illegal confession? Cause I'm about to admit to killing Kennedy if you keep talking to me."

The officer shakes her head but doesn't say anything else to Tineshia for the rest of the ride..

At the precinct, Tineshia is processed. The officer takes Tineshia's prints, then sits her down with a lady detective.

"All right now, before I start all this paperwork, is there anything you would like to say or any statement you would like to make?" asks the lady detective.

"I am under 18 you not allowed to ask me any questions. I already told your partner here I want to call my parents. I know my rights." Tineshia says defiantly.

The detective and officer look at each other. "I already know, I had to deal with this the whole ride here." the lady officer remarks.

The detective scoffs. "Go ahead and take her to make her phone call. Then put her in interrogation five. She is obviously not going to make this easy on herself, I don't need her sitting infront of me while I fill this out."

Tineshia dials her Dad's phone number. "Daddy it's me. I been arrested."

"We already know and are on our way, everything is going to be ok. Are you ok baby?"

"I'm confused and scared Daddy." Tineshia says whimpering. "They are talking about pressing charges and witnesses and..."

"Stay strong baby. Don't let them scare you. We talked about what to do if you were ever falsely accused remember? Don't say anything until we get there. No need to be scared when you know you haven't done anything wrong. I love you. Its all going to be ok."

Tineshia straightens up. "Yes Daddy I remember. I love you too. I'll see you soon." Tineshia hangs up the phone.

"Aww that was sweet. Come on." the lady officer takes Tineshia to interrogation.

Tineshia is sitting alone in the dark grey room handcuffed to the table. Her adrenaline has come down, dressed only in a black tank top and skirt that stops just above her knees, not only is she nervous but now cold. She feels like she has been waiting forever. She looks around the room but only sees grey walls, the steel rectangular table, one door to her right, and what she suspects is a two-way mirror directly in-front of her.

Behind the two-way mirror is a male detective and a well-dressed older white man who is reading thru Tineshia's file. The door opens to the observation room and a woman detective enters.

"The ADA is on his way, and her parents are here."

"ADA? Call him and tell him he can go back to bed" says the mysterious gentleman. He pulls out his phone and makes a call. "I don't know why, I am hearing one of your assistants were in route, but I sent them home. I expect to see you here in the next 15 minutes." The gentleman hangs up the phone. Go ahead and let her family in, maybe I can finally find out who broke my niece's jaw. Since the police department's finest let the other girl get away."

The male detective exits the room and escorts Tineshia's parents to the interrogation room. The door opens and in comes her mother Betty Wite, 5'10 and mocha complected, 41 years old wearing jeans and a sweater. Along with Betty is Tineshia's father, 47 year old coffee complected, 6'6 280lb John Wite wearing a black bomber jacket, tee-shirt, and sweat pants . Betty has a look of concern in her eyes "Baby, are you okay? What happened?" She runs to hug and hold Tineshia.

John with anger in his voice, "Why the hell is she still handcuffed? What the hell is going on? Get those cuffs off her now! John takes off his jacket and places it around his Tineshia's shoulders.

The detective comes in and takes the cuffs off. "I'm detective Tim. I was informed you did not want to make a statement without your parents. Your parents are here now. Are you prepared to make a statement?"

The DA, in a rush and breathing heavy, enters the observation room with the lady detective and the mysterious gentleman.

"I was in route, just thought my ADA would be here sooner, anyway where are we? Have they made any statements?

"Shh" says the mysterious gentleman and turns up the volume on the intercom.

"Our lawyer is on the way." John says

"Oh, you all have a lawyer?"

"What do you mean, "Oh, you all have a lawyer?" Yes, we got a lawyer. Matter of fact, we would like some time alone with our daughter please and thank you. And make sure there are no recording devices on, please." The detective laughs under his breath and walks out the room.

"I want to know who their lawyer is and his background" says the mysterious gentleman.

The lady detective reaches for the volume control on the intercom.

"Just what in the hell, do you think you doing?"

"They asked for a lawyer. We can't talk to them or listen in on their conversations until after they speak to their attorney."

"Sweet cheeks, you and our soon to be former DA run along and get the information I asked for. Oh, and bring me a coffee black. Thank you."

The lady detective and the DA leave the observation room, While the gentleman stays and continues to listen to the Wite family's conversation.

"T what the hell happened?" Betty asks. Zahra came home and told us you had been arrested and was telling me y'all were in a fight or something?"

"Mommy, it wasn't my fault. I tried to stop it. It just got out of hand real quick."

"Baby, are you okay?" asks her father.

"Yes, Daddy I'm okay. I'm just cold and so tired. What time is it? "Where is Ty and Tye (Tineshia's thirteen-year-old twin nephew and niece)?"

"It is 5:30 a.m. baby. Did they charge you with anything? He leans in and whispers, Ty and Tye are in the car asleep with Zahra. Now, how did Zahra get away? Do they know about her?"

"No, no. I don't think they know about her. She was way ahead of me when I fell."

Betty says, "You fell? How'd you fall? And Z ain't help you? Thought she was supposed to be your 'best friend'?" Betty makes air quotation marks.

"No. She stopped and was going to come back. I told her no and to keep running."

John sits on the table. "Okay baby, tell me what happened. Is anybody dead?"

Tineshia jumps back in her seat. "*Dead? NO!* Ain't nobody dead!"

John makes a hand gesture. "Okay, baby, keep it down. Tell me what happened.

"We ain't even start anything. We were leaving the party; these three white girls came out of nowhere. They tried to challenge us in a dance battle or something, I don't know. All I know is they were drunk as fuck."

"Watch your mouth hunny." Betty says.

John cuts his eyes at his wife. "Really, Betty?"

Betty snaps her head round to John "Yes, really. Just cause we in a police station, doesn't mean she gets to act like she doesn't have any manners."

"Anyways, like I was saying...."

Betty turns back to Tineshia "*Anyway!* Who you think you talking to?"

"Betty please" says John. Betty puts her hands up and head down.

Tineshia continues. "So, they were drunk, trying to dance, and Zahra and I couldn't help it, we just started laughing. One of the girls got mad and talked about Z's dad."

"Shit," Betty says.

John clears his throat. "Language, Betty.". Betty gives John a look.

Tineshia starts again. "Yeah, so I knew things were about to go left, so I tried to hold her back, but one of them stomped on my foot...see." Tineshia points at the mark on her shoe. Which made me let go of Z, so she knocked one of the girls out, then the other two tried to jump her so I jumped in and next thing all three of them were on the ground and the police were there. We started to run but my foot was still hurt, so that's why I fell, but Z was able to get away."

"Aight," says John. "so this was just a little scuffle, but nobody was seriously hurt, so you going be okay baby. Don't worry."

"Were you smoking?" asks Betty

"No Ma. We had a few drinks, but no, we don't smoke."

Betty hugs Tineshia and stokes her hair. "Okay baby, okay. It's going to be okay"

Observation room door opens, the DA returns to the room. He hands the gentleman a folder.

"Their lawyer's name is Samuel Leaf. He's a private attorney has about 10 clients. Handles mostly low-level misdemeanors, bar fights, assaults, simple drug possessions." The gentleman doesn't say a word.

The interrogation door opens, and in walks Tim with Sam. "Your lawyer is here. Knock on the glass when y'all are ready."

Sam reaches his hand out. "Betty, John, Tineshia how are you?"

"Ready to go home." replies Tineshia. Sam sits down.

"I bet. Tell me what happened and let's see what we can do about getting you out of here." Sam pulls out a pad and pen.

John begins: "It was just a little fight, and they started it." Sam interrupts.

"John, I need to hear from her what happened...no disrespect." Tineshia looks at her father. John nods his head.

"I was just leaving a party and these drunk girls were disrespectful to us, and one of them bumped into me and that started the little fight."

"So first off do you have any prior arrests?"

"No, I don't"

"Great. So, secondly, you said we? Do they have anyone else in custody?"

"No. I was at the party with my best friend Zahra, but when we ran, she got away, but I couldn't cause one the girls stomped on my foot."

"Okay so it was two of you, and you tried to run but one got away. So, you were at a party. Were you drinking or did you have any drugs? They're probably going to order a tox report, so I need you to be a hundred percent honest with me."

"No drugs, but yes, we had a few drinks, but we were not drunk."

"Great." says Sam as he continues to take notes. "Okay, so these drunk girls. Were they classmates? Were they visibly drunk at the party where others could see them? Have you or your friend had run ins with them in the past?

"No, they weren't at the party. They had gotten out of a car across the street. I have never seen them before or know where they came from."

"Oh okay, so they weren't even from the party." Sam goes back through his notes. "So, last question. What race were these girls?

Tineshia looks confused. "Why does that matter? They were white."

"Shit!" blurts out Betty as she puts her hand over her head.

The detectives enter the observation room. Tim looks at the DA, "So, how hard are we pressing this?"

"If you will shut the fuck up. I will let you know." states the mysterious gentleman.

Sam asks Tineshia, "Okay so this Zahra, is she willing to turn herself in? Make a statement?"

"They don't know about her, and I don't want to get her jammed up if possible."

"Okay, so we got underage drinking, assault, and evading arrest."

"*Excuse me!* Betty bursts out. "Exactly whose side are you on? We're the ones paying you, ain't it? What the hell is this?"

"I'm sorry. Let me explain how I like to work. I like to collect information and try to predict how the prosecution would come at us. This is not me placing blame at all. So, Tineshia is there anything else I need to know? Anything at all?"

"That's about it other than the lil officer trying to coax info out me, thinking she could call me sister and I would just start gabbing to her."

"Was this before or after you asked for a lawyer?"

"Both actually."

Sam finishes writing "Alright, I'm going to go ahead and call them in here, okay? Just let me do all the talking, okay family?" Tineshia nods, Sam looks at John and Betty.

"Yes, you do all the talking." Responds Betty.

Sam stands up and proceeds to knock on the glass.

Tim turns to the DA. "So, what we thinking here? Threaten her with second degree assault? Let her plead down? Thousand hour of community service and a fine?

"Sounds about..." The gentleman interrupts.

"What sounds right? My niece is in the hospital right now, getting her jaw wired shut! You're suggesting community service?

"I figured you would be pursing them for damages in civil court."

The gentleman gives a hard look at the DA. Then looks at the detectives. "The charge is aggravated assault and attempted robbery."

"Aggravated assault and attempted robbery?" Asks Trish. "From every witness account, including your niece, this was a silly fight. And this little girl, wasn't even the one who started it or hit your niece?"

The gentleman steps past the DA, towards the detectives. He hands the folders in his hands to Trish and looks back at the DA. "I want this friend of hers, Zahra. If she wants any type of deal...she will have to give up her friend. I am on my way to the hospital. Call me and let me know what she decides." The gentleman turns and walks out the room.

After the door closes. "Okay, who the hell is that guy?" Trish asks.

"You don't want to know his name or who he is, trust me." Responds the DA. "The charge is aggravated assault and attempted robbery. If she does not give up her friend...she does not go home tonight."

Tim enters the interrogation room with his partner, Trish. "We all caught up now and ready?" Tim asks. The two detectives sit down, turn on a recorder, and pull out notepads and pens.

Sam says, "Yes, this was a small altercation between young kids. My client apologizes for her role in this. She promises not to do anything like this again and is contrite."

"Do again? I ain't even..." Sam looks at Tineshia as if to say *be quiet*, and John puts his hand on her shoulder. Trish and Tim snicker.

"My client has no record and is a good kid. It's late. Let's just put this whole thing to bed, okay?"

Tim and Trish finish writing. Tim smiles. "She's sorry, huh? See we, starting off in the wrong way. How am I to believe anything you tell me, counselor? Your own client couldn't even keep a straight face while you told that lie."

"Look, detective.." Begins Sam

"No, you look counsel. I don't care how late it is, this ain't going to bed anytime soon, you understand? Now your client is being charged with aggravated assault and attempted robbery."

Betty quickly stands up. John takes his hand off Tineshia's shoulder and steps forward. Tineshia scrunches her face with a look of disbelief. "*WHAT?*" cries Betty.

"Just what the hell y'all trying to pull here?" John says.

Trish stands up. "I suggest you have a seat, ma'am, and you both calm down." Betty folds her arms and stares down the detective. John stands tall.

"Now, as I was saying." Tim says. "You are being charged with aggravated assault and attempted robbery. We have a witness, on top of the three girls you and your accomplice beat up and tried to steal from." Tineshia starts to cry. Betty sits back down and hugs her daughter. "Now, if you give us the name of your accomplice and confess, I will take it to the DA and let them know you're cooperating."

"This is bogus and outrageous." Sam exclaims. "My client didn't assault anyone. She was minding her business when those three girls accosted her. They stomped on her foot...she has the mark on her shoe and limp to prove it."

"We have witnesses that say otherwise and that she got the mark on her shoe when she tried to step to one of the girls. Not to mention we have two officers who saw her accomplice try to flee." Says Trish. She looks at Tineshia, folds her arms, and shakes her head. "See, if you weren't trying to ghetto stomp those poor girls maybe you wouldn't have hurt your foot and you wouldn't have gotten caught, like your friend." Tineshia puts her head onto her mother's chest sobbing.

John says, "What the fuck you mean, ghetto stomp? Who you think you are? Just who do you think you talking to?"

"Sir," says Tim. "We already told you to calm down once. We won't say it again. I suggest you let your"... he clears his throat..."lawyer do the talking for y'all."

"We categorically deny all these false charges." says Sam firmly.

"So, she doesn't want to give us the name of her partner in crime?" Tim shrugs, stands up and opens the door, and gestures towards an officer outside. "Officer, cuff her, please, and take her down to processing. She will be arraigned later this morning." The officer steps into the room and forcibly stands Tineshia up.

"Daddy!.."

John reaches out towards the officer. Tim steps in and forces John to back up.

"Mommy!" Betty reaches her hand out towards her now, handcuffed daughter. The officer walks Tineshia out of the room. Betty holds her head while tears run down her face.

Over the next few months, the charges led to an indictment. The indictment led to a trial and now the trial is over, and Tineshia has been found guilty of assault and attempted robbery. She is in court awaiting sentencing.

"You have been found guilty, and I am sentencing you to five years in prison." The sound of the judge's voice fades out. John hugs Betty, who is sobbing. Ty and Tye are standing next to Betty, looking up at her. Tineshia is crying as the court officer comes to escort her out of court. She looks out at her family and reaches towards John. The DA stands up and shakes his assistant's hand. The court officer forcibly guides Tineshia out of the court room.

CHAPTER 3

THE FAMILY YOU CHOOSE

The prison gates open. Tineshia, now twenty-two years old and grown to 6'2 now, is standing there, holding her property in a bag. Her parents are standing at the gate, overly excited. Betty runs toward her daughter and gives her a huge hug. Her dad comes up and hugs the both of them. Quietly, they walk to the car. Music is playing and her parents are talking, but Tineshia zones out as she stares out the window, noticing all the changes. When they arrive home, she walks to her house and opens the door.

"Welcome home!" A crowd of her friends and family is awaiting her. There is a cookout in her honor. The first person to run up and hug her is Zahra who now 6'.

Towards the end of the party, Zahra and Tineshia are alone. "So what's your plan?" asks Zahra.

"Honestly all I been thinking about is finishing school and trying to get my degree. I'm twenty-two now and feel like I'm so far behind. I mean, look at you."

"Well, I'm lucky." Zahra replies. "My dad's life insurance allowed my mom and I some financial freedom and to open the coffee shop. So I was able to learn and work under her before she got sick."

Tineshia puts her hand on Zahra's leg. "I know how you and your mother helped us out when I first went away." Zahra hugs Tineshia. "I love you so much." Exclaims Tineshia. "And from what you told me last visitation, sounded like you are running the place."

"I mean." With a smirk Zahra says. "My mom can rarely come in anymore, so yeah. The staff all knows me as the boss. So, I was thinking, what better way to get you some real-world experience than for you to come work with your girl?"

Tineshia has a look of shock on her face. "You can do that?"

"Like you said, I'm running the place. Tell your parole board or deputy or whoever you got a real job. You can be, like, my assistant or whatever and we can reconnect. Get some money in your pocket, flexible hours...I mean, what better boss can you have than me?" Zahra looks innocently. Tineshia smiles and gives her friend a hug.

Three months have gone by, Tineshia is enrolled in community college and working full time at Zahra's family coffee shop. On her break, sitting at an empty table with a laptop and a book open. William Johnson II, a cleanly dressed 6'5 and fit thirty-seven year old blond haired white man, notices Tineshia and one of the books she has in-front of her.

"You're probably going to need something stronger than coffee to help you with that one." He remarks.

Tineshia without looking up from her typing, says with a look of annoyance on her face, "Please c'mon. That's the best line you got?" She finishes typing and looks up, and her facial expression changes from annoyance to embarrassment, "I'm sorry sir." She starts stuttering "I...I...thought you."

"I mean, what makes you think I wasn't?" William says as he sips his coffee. Tineshia smiles. "It feels like just yesterday I tortured myself through these very subjects."

"Oh, you studied law?" asks Tineshia.

"I've dabbled."

"Well, if you say you remember these books, that will mean you would be a trial attorney?"

"Yes, I specialized in trial and contract law."

"That's what's up!" Tineshia says. "Any advice you want to give me?"

"Don't." They both laugh. "Just realize we all tend to get into this field with the best intentions, but those we have to use our knowledge for don't always have those same good intentions."

"Hmm, that's deep." responds Tineshia.

"May I ask, what is your motivation to take this on? Or you just like torture?" William asks.

Tineshia sighs. "That's a long story."

"Well, if now is not the time, maybe we can meet up and discuss this further later." William says. Tineshia blushes, sneaking a peek at the gentleman's left hand, noticing a wedding ring.

"I don't know if you really want to do that." She lifts her pants leg and shows him her ankle monitor. "And would your wife be okay with that?"

"Oh, now I'm really interested to know the story...and what makes you assume it's a wife?" William raises his eyebrows. "I'm going to leave you my card, and if you would like to tell me more or ask me anything else, by all means give me a call." He pulls out his card, winks at Tineshia, and walks out the coffee shop. Tineshia takes the card and smiles, as she watches him walk away.

Zahra, who was watching the entire scenario via cameras in her office, comes from the back over to her friend. "Was that what I thought it was?"

"What you talking about?" asks Tineshia.

"Girl, don't even try to play me. He come in every day, but he ain't never paid any of the girls any attention. Marci a 25 year old busty white woman with green eyes, Zahra's second in charge at the café, been pushing her DD cleavage and smiling all in his face. She thought he was gay."

Tineshia rolls her eyes and laughs. "Well, I don't think he gay, or maybe he's bi? I don't know. It seems like he was flirting, though. I don't know; he was a little vague, but I think he's married or something."

Zahra "Uh huh...did you give him your number? That's the real question.

"It wasn't even like that, though. He just noticed me studying and said he remembered when he was in class and all."

Zahra leans in and whispers. "Bitch, did he get your digits?"

Tineshia scrunches her face and smirks. “No....I got his card, though.” Tineshia and Zahra both chuckle. “But I ain’t got time for no drama or whatever. You can tell he a lawyer. He dodged all my questions and shit.”

“T, you better call that man. He is cute. You talking about you ain’t got time.” Zahra rolls her eyes. “Talking about you ain’t got time...shit, if he married, then you ain’t got to worry about no time. Shit, he a lawyer, you know he got a few coins, so he gay or not, he can put you on.” Tineshia starts twirling William II’s business card and thinking. Zahra snatches the card from her hand. “William Johnson II, huh? Sound like he a boss or something. You look him up yet?”

Tineshia reaches for the card. “No, girl give me that.”

“Ain’t you studying? You worry about studying them books and I’ll study Sir William.” Tineshia sucks her teeth. Zahra pulls out her phone and proceeds to google William II’s name. “Oh, girl.” Zahra hands Tineshia her phone. “He not just a boss, he the head of his own firm.” Tineshia scrolls through intensely. “Shit if Brandon (Zahra’s Boyfriend) ain’t watch so much *Law and Order and First 48*, I would have you set up a double date with one of his partners.”

Tineshia laughs. “You better stop playing with Brandon, You know he ain’t with the games.”

“You Brandon’s biggest fan, always defending him and shit. You supposed to be with me when I’m trying to do my ratchet shit." Zahra sticks out her tongue and does a little dance. Zahra and Tineshia burst out laughing. "Matter of fact, ain't your break over? Don't make me tell your boss." Tineshia laughs, stands up, and snatches William II's card from Zahra.

"Aight, aight, I got you." She picks up her stuff and gets back to work.

CHAPTER 4

A NEW DOOR

Two days later, it's Friday. Tineshia is lying down in her room, staring at the ceiling. She picks up her phone and texts Zahra.

“Hey, girl”, responds Zahra.

“Hey, Z. what you up to?” asks Tineshia.

“Just in the room packing, Brandon sweeping me away for the weekend. What’s good?” responds Zahra.

“See I told you stop playing with that man.” says Tineshia.

Zahra sends an eye roll emoji. “He probably feeling guilty about something. I’m about to get him to tell on himself on the ride. What you got going on?”

"You always at that boy neck. I was just thinking of some moves, but everybody seems busy." Tineshia says disappointed.

"It's like 7:30, girl, you know you can't be playing with them people. You got to be in the house by like 9:00, ain't it?" Zahra asks.

"Yeah, today is a wrap," Tineshia replies. "I was looking more about tomorrow or maybe a brunch Sunday."

"Well, we will be back Sunday afternoon. We can do an early dinner or something?" suggests Zahra.

"It's cool, I'll figure something out." says Tineshia. "You just have fun, girl, and don't stress that man out."

"It's been two years with this man's foolishness. He don't just do no romantic shit out of the blue. He up to something or fucked up something. Either way I'm going to find the shit out." exclaims Zahra.

Tineshia sends an "laughing face emoji."

Tineshia plays music and scrolls through her phone for a while. It's now 8:30 and Tineshia is at her desk in her room going through her purse. She finds William's business card. She twirls the card in her hand and thinks for a minute, before picking up her phone and starting to text.

"Hi, William. this is Tineshia."

"Tineshia?" asks William?

"Yes, the lawyer/waitress from the coffee shop."

William sends a smiley face emoji. "Ahh yes, the lady with the complicated story. How are you this evening?"

"I'm good. How are you? Hope it's not too late?" Tineshia asks.

"Late....it's not even 10 yet. I thought I would be the elder statesman here." William asks.

Tineshia sends a laughing emoji. "Anyway, I was wondering if your offer to mentor is still open."

"Was that what I offered?" says William, followed by a thinking emoji. "Thought you were going to be filling me in on somethings."

"Nah counsel."

"Uh huh... well, I'm out of town right now, but how about we have brunch Sunday, and we can further debate whose recollection is correct?" William suggests.

"I'm right, but I will allow you to take me to brunch as an apology for being wrong" responds Tineshia.

William sends another laughing emoji. "Okay, Ms. Lady, should I pick you up or do you want to meet me?"

"I'll meet you there." Tineshia says.

"Okay, I'll text you the address. Let's say about 2?" asks William.

"That works... see you then." Tineshia responds.

It's 1:50 p.m. on Sunday. Tineshia is riding the elevator when the elevator dings, Tineshia is turned around, the elevator has stopped but the door she walked in didn't open. She looks around and notices it was another set of doors behind her that are now open. She looks around, half way embarrassed, to see if anyone noticed, then steps off the hotel elevator. She looks left and right. William notices her and stands up so she can see him. Tineshia catches sight of him and smiles and walks towards his table. He pulls the chair out for her to sit down.

"Oh, why thank you and they say chivalry is dead."

William smiles. "You look amazing."

"Thank you."

"Have you been here before?" asks William.

"No, I can't say that I have. This is a nice hotel. I didn't know they did brunch here."

"That's what I like...they have great food and music while still being low-key, you know?" Tineshia smiles.

Quietly, Tineshia and William order food, eat, talk and laugh. During the conversation, Tineshia lifts up the bottom of her dress to expose her ankle monitor. Towards the end of the meal and before the check comes.

"You have experienced a lot for someone so young" remarks William.

"Hmm, experienced...that's an interesting way to put it. Almost makes it seem like I had a choice." Tineshia responds.

"No, that is not what I meant to convey. More of admiration for your resilience at life's attempts to hold you back. That is a quality I think most people never develop, probably because they never have to."

"Admiration, huh? So, you are...what? Proud of me?" Tineshia asks confused.

The server brings the check and William hands them his card without taking a look at it. "Yes, but I wouldn't say I'm proud of you...more that you make me proud. The majority of people I'm around and work with are one mistake, misfortune, life event away from being ready to just give up. You, though... your head stays high and your aura and vibe suggest to me that no matter what, you are not only going to survive, but you are going to thrive. And look flawless as you do it." William winks at Tineshia.

Tineshia blushes. "You have all the answers, huh?"

"No, just all the questions." William responds.

Tineshia laughs. "Alright, now Taye Diggs. I've seen Love Jones as well."

William leans in. "So, you know what happens next, then, right?"

Tineshia frowns. "Uh...what you think comes next?"

William stands up and walks towards Tineshia. "Now I get you to dance with me." He reaches out his hand for Tineshia's.

She smiles and grabs his hand. "Don't try and touch my butt, now."

"That's a different movie."

They walk towards the dance floor. The music grows louder as they get closer. The DJ has a slow song playing. Tineshia and William dance closely together and looking at each other intensely. The song ends and they back away from each other slowly. The music changes to the Electric Slide. People rush onto the floor in excitement. William starts smiling and gets a very excited youthful look on his face. Tineshia has a look of a shock and amazement. William joins the crowd doing the Electric Slide. Tineshia watches him dance, smiling and covering her face. He dances enthusiastically.

Tineshia gets a call from Zahra. She steps away, while keeping an eye on William. "Hello."

"T, girl, where you at? We almost back. What's all that noise?" asks Zahra.

"Hey, Z, I'm out at brunch."

"You at brunch? Oooh...who you on a date with?"

"Who said I was on a date?"

"Uh huh...okay, girl, I get it. You ain't got none in... what, four years now? I ain't mad at you."

"It ain't even like that." Tineshia continues to protest.

"Yeah, yeah. Get off the phone with me and have some fun. Call me after. Bye!"

"Girl bye."

The music changes to the Cupid Shuffle. William comes and grabs Tineshia's hand and pulls her towards the dance floor. They start doing the dance together. After the second chorus. Tineshia pulls William off the dance floor and back towards their table, laughing the whole way. "I haven't danced in a long time" she says.

"That smile, though... wow. Truly stunning." William remarks.

Tineshia is left speechless and blushing. William mistakes the look on her face for confusion and thinking he may have said something wrong, asks "What?"

"So, what's your plan now. Taye Diggs? According to the movie, I guess you're supposed to walk me home. Try and get me to invite you in, or something, right?

"Well, I'd like to switch from the movie in this instance." William pulls out a room key and sets it on the table.

"Hmm...and what movie is this from?" asks Tineshia.

William smiles. "My company helped fund the development of this hotel, and for that, we were given the penthouse here. I would like you to choose to meet me in the penthouse, but whether you choose to or not. Monday, you have a paid internship as a paralegal as you continue your education." He stands up, kisses Tineshia on the forehead, and walks towards the elevator.

Tineshia is left to contemplate as she sits there and plays with the room key.

CHAPTER 5

LIVE AGAIN

There is a knock on the penthouse door. William struts towards the door and looks through the peep hole, then his facial expression changes. He opens the door. It's room service. "I didn't order anything," he says.

"Yes, sir, a lady ordered this at the lobby and asked us to deliver this note."

William receives the note and a bucket. "Was there supposed to be a bottle with this?"

"This and the note is what I was given, sir. Have a good evening."

William opens the note. It reads. "You may need the ice along with the next delivery."

There is another knock at the door. William turns back and opens. "What did she send this time?" he mutters to himself.

When the door opens Tineshia is standing in the hallway. "Herself" she says and walks in.

William has a huge grin on his face. "Now. I don't want you to...."

Tineshia interrupts. "What makes you think this was your decision?" She presses and pins him against the wall and kissing him passionately. Tineshia runs her hands up his leg until she reaches his cock and gives a gentle squeeze. Tineshia turns and walks towards the bed, taking off the shoulder straps of her dress as she walks. By the time Tineshia gets to the bed her dress is off and she sits down on the bed with her matching bra and panties. William walks over to Tineshia. As he gets closer Tineshia leans back in the bed and lifts her right leg out hitting William in his thigh and stopping him. William drops to his knees. When William gets on his knees, he kisses her knee and slowly slides his hand up Tineshia's leg. Once William reaches Tineshia's panties, he slides them down and pulls Tineshia to the edge of the bed. William starts kissing his way up Tineshia's inner thigh. Tineshia palms the back of Williams head as he begins to kiss her other set of lips. Tineshia moans and squirms in pleasure.

"Fuck!" Tineshia moans, after about fifteen minutes.

Tineshia's thighs squeeze around William's head. William stops and stands up.

"Do you have a condom?" asks Tineshia. William reaches in his pocket and pulls out a golden packet containing a condom. As William uses his teeth to open the packet, Tineshia unbuckles and pulls down his pants and underwear. She cups his balls with one hand and strokes his cock with the other. William puts the condom on and Tineshia scoots back to the middle of the bed. William steps out of his pants that now lay at his ankles, then climbs on to the bed, on top of Tineshia. William leans in and kisses Tineshia again. While kissing William Tineshia flips him onto his back and mounts him. She grabs him and slides him inside her. Tineshia closes her eyes and smirks as she feels him and sits her hips down to feel him deeper. She places her hands on his chest as she rides William. He puts his hands on her ass as he holds on for the ride. Tineshia starts slowly rolling her hips, but gradually increases the voracity and aggressiveness causing William to moan.

"Fuck!" William shouts as Tineshia has brought him to climax. After they've finished, Tineshia starts getting dressed.

"Mmmm...so you just going to do me like that and leave?" William asks. "Starting to feel like another movie. Am I going to find some money on a dresser or table somewhere?"

"You definitely don't have to worry about that." She

points towards her ankle. "It's already eight p.m. I have about an hour to get back around my way. At least, for next six months; I got a curfew."

William sits up on the side of the bed "Ahh, that sucks, but that's probably best. I need to build up my endurance to handle any more of that."

Tineshia is getting dressed and looking for her bra. "Anymore, huh? So, you think you getting more?"

William picks up the bra that is on the floor by his feet, and waves it for her to see. Tineshia smiles, smacks her head, and walks towards him. She reaches for the bra. William II grabs her hand and pulls her close to him. "Yes, I think there should be more." He lightly strokes her cheek and grabs her chin and pulls her in for a kiss. After the kiss he looks deeply into her eyes and whispers, "And I think you, think so too."

Tineshia bites her lip and smiles. She whispers, "I got to go" and slowly pulls away. She puts her bra in her purse and starts to put on her shoes.

"How far away are you?" asks William. "Did you drive?"

"I'm about thirty minutes away, and no. I caught a Lyft I don't have my own car yet. That's why I'm moving so quickly, I gotta get back on time."

"Ahh, okay. I was feeling some type of way, that you popped up so quickly after we were done."

Tineshia looks back at William and smiles. "Oh, I have a feeling I'm going to sleep well tonight."

William stands up, picks up his phone, and sends a message. Tineshia starts walking towards the door, William right behind her. She gets to the door, turns around, and gives William a peck kiss. As she tries to turn back towards the door, he grabs her and pulls her in closely for a passionate kiss.

"I got to go." Tineshia whispers.

"I'm pretty sure you going to make it in time." William takes his hands off Tineshia. She smiles, opens the door, and leaves.

Tineshia gets off the elevator on the lobby floor with her phone in her hand. As she is walking towards the door, she is pulling up the Lyft app to order her ride. Outside, a man greets her. "Ms. Wite?"

"Excuse me, do I know you?" Tineshia asks confused as to how this stranger knows her name.

"No, ma'am, not yet anyway. My name is Chad (6'6, bald with a goatee, muscular black man) I am Mr. Johnson's driver. I was told you were in a hurry. I would like to offer you a ride." He gestures towards an all-black luxury vehicle, walks to the back passenger door, and opens it. Tineshia blushes and walks towards the car.

"Thank you." Chad closes the door and walks around towards the driver's door.

CHAPTER 6

TEA TIME

As the car is pulling up to Tineshia's parents' house, she notices Zahra is sitting on the porch. Chad pulls the car over and comes around and opens the door to let Tineshia step out.

"Thank you, Chad."

"Have a good evening, Ms. Wite."

Tineshia walks towards the house.

"You cutting it close, aren't you?" exclaims Zahra, while looking down at her watch. "And since when Lyft start sending cars like that? I must be paying you too much. You out here splurging on Lyft blacks for a damn brunch and shit."

Tineshia laughs and starts to open the door "That's not a Lyft and umm, starting Monday, I don't think I work for you anymore."

"Excuse me! You quitting me?"

When Tineshia opens the door John is standing there. "Tineshia, you had us worried its eight-fifty p.m." he says.

"I'm sorry, Daddy, I should have called you."

John walks towards Tineshia and kisses her on the forehead. "Baby, you're grown and I trust you. You ain't got to report to me, but you have less than six months left. Then you're officially done with this bullshit."

"I know, Daddy, I will be careful and won't cut it so close again. Where is Mommy?

"Like mother like daughter, I guess, she still out with her girls. At least, she hit me though. She said she'd be home in a minute. Zahra, was this you that got her out cutting it so close to her curfew?"

"No, Mr. Wite. I...." Zahra begins. Tineshia looks at her. "I mean, sir, I tried to set my alarm to remind me of the time, but we were dancing and must didn't hear it go off."

John shakes his head. "Y'all going to make me start chaperoning, and I know y'all don't want that."

Tineshia hugs John. "I'm sorry Daddy. Won't happen again."

"Mm hmm." John walks away.

Zahra drags Tineshia to her room. She pulls Tineshia forcibly in and shuts the door. "Now, bitch, tell me what's going on! Why I just lie to your dad? And what the hell you mean, you not working with me anymore? Who the hell were you with? *What the hell is going on*?"

Tineshia starts laughing "Damn, the police ain't question me like this." She sits down on her bed.

"T!"

"Okay, okay, so, you remember when I text you and said I wanted to do something this weekend?"

"Yeah. That's when I told you Brandon wanted to be fake romantic and shit. Have rose petals on the bed and shit. I mean, it was cute or whatever, but..."

"Z! Do you want to hear what happened or not?"

"My bad, my bad. I'm listening.

"So yeah, after you told me you were going to be busy,

I was going through my purse and..., I.....Just so happen....to find that business card from William Johnson."

Zahra sits down on the bed next to Tineshia. "Ahh shit."

"Yeah, so he was like, let's meet for brunch Sunday. And girl....the man is smooth. I mean, not the swag but smooth as shit." Zahra starts laughing. "I'm serious, Z., electric slide came on and this man on the floor getting' it, you hear me?"

"Oh so old man got some rhythm, huh?"

"Girl he not that old, but yes, or he got a little cousin teaching him moves or something, I mean they played cupid shuffle and he dragged me up on the dance floor and was moving."

"Hold up, electric slide and cupid shuffle? So, this must have been towards the end?"

"Yeah, it was about the time you called me." Tineshia says.

"Bitch, that was five-thirty. If they were starting to close up at five-thirty, why you just now getting home?" Tineshia turns her head and starts blushing. "T, I know, I know you ain't sleep with him."

Tineshia "I mean, you were the one who told me have a good time, right?"

"*Tineshia*! I ain't know you was out with a sugar daddy and shit."

Zahra and Tineshia laugh. "The man has game Z. He had me opening up to him and everything." Zahra looks shocked and amazed. "I know, you know I don't even like talking to people like that." Tineshia continues. "Then next thing I know, he sliding me the penthouse room key and telling me I got a job at his law firm."

"Oh hell no, hold up you ain't go like that."

Tineshia has a look of disrespect on her face. "Fuck, you mean. You should know me better than that. He ain't proposition me."

"That's what I know. My bad." says Zahra.

"I said ole boy was smooth. He gave me the job period. It had nothing to do with me going to his room or not."

"So, you didn't go?" Zahra asks with raised eyebrows.

Tineshia goes quiet and avoids Zahra's gaze.

Zahra moves her head to make eye contact. "So, you didn't go, right!"

Tineshia lowers her head and whispers. “I did.”

Zahra jumps off the bed. “HOE! “She starts dancing and singing “Hoe, you’s a hoe, *hoe*, you’s a hoe, I said that you’s a hoe, *hoe*.”

“Girl, fuck you.”

Zahra sits back down. “It’s okay, girl. You been out of it for a while. He ran some good game on you.”

“Whatever. Fuck you. Z.”

Zahra starts laughing, then stops “Hold up, thought you said he was married or gay or something? Didn’t you say he had a ring on?”

Tineshia stands up and starts putting things away. “Look, I’m pretty sure he not gay. You feel me, after what just went down.”

“Shit, girl, like I said you been out the game for a minute. A lot of these men now-a-days go both ways.” Zahra says as she rolls her eyes.

“Well, I don’t think he gay, and if he married, that’s his problem, you feel me? If he ain’t showing respect to his marriage, that’s on him. I ain’t go out looking for him, he came for me, you know? I'm not looking for anything long term or anything just some relief right now, you know."

"Well damn, aight now. I stand corrected, playa playa."

There is a knock at the door. Tineshia shouts, "Yeah?"

"Can I come in?" It's Tye's voice. Zahra opens the door. Tye, 17 year old 5'5 light skin girl with a curly bush, hugs Zahra tightly. "Hey Auntie Z. I thought I heard your voice."

"Uh huh, I bet," Tineshia says. "You better not been eaves dropping outside my door."

Tye goes and hugs Tineshia. "No, T, I told you I wouldn't do that anymore. Why, what y'all talking about? You finally get you a man?" Zahra starts laughing.

"What you mean, finally? I ain't even been home that long. I ain't running after none of these dudes out here." exclaims Tineshia.

"Shit, I don't know, T. If I wasn't around a man for four years, I'd be out here, you hear me?" Tye starts dancing. Zahra and Tye laugh. Tineshia shakes her head.

"Little girl, you barely seventeen what you know about it?"

"First of all, I am almost eighteen and I am full grown. And B.

Zahra interrupts. B?

Tye laughs. Tineshia used to do that when I was a kid. She would say first of all, then B, then third. I thought it was cute so I started doing it too. Anyway shit, girl, bae already know. He be blowing my phone up. I don't play that shit. I don't hear from you. To the streets I go, you feel me?"

Zahra starts laughing. Tineshia shakes her head. "Don't feed into her, Z. Shit, she starting to sound like you. I can tell y'all spent way too much time together, while I was gone." Zahra and Tye hug.

"When my parents died," says Tye. "Aunt B and Uncle John adopted my brother and me. You know I was all up under you those first few years, but when you went away. Aunty Z came over almost every day to check on me." Tineshia, Zahra and Tye have a group hug.

"Where your hard-headed brother at. anyway?" asks Tineshia.

"Shit, I don't know. Probably in the streets trying to run game on some poor girl."

"I thought twins were supposed to be able to sense each other or whatever." says Zahra.

"I don't know nothing about that. Maybe that's for identical twins."

"Well, I need both of you to go about your business." I need to take a shower and get some rest. I got a new job to get ready for in the morning." She sticks out her tongue.

"Uh huh. I'm sure you killed your interview today, huh?" says Zahra as she smiles and walks towards the door.

Tineshia throws a pillow at her. "Get out." Zahra grabs Tye and pulls her out the room.

"What interview? Who interviews on Sunday's?" Tye asks. The door closes.

CHAPTER 7

BALANCING OF THE SCALES

It is 9:55 am on Thursday, and Tineshia is at her desk, typing on the computer. Her new supervisor Stephanie, a 55 year old 5'4 white lady with glasses, drops a stack of papers on her desk. "These need to be filled out no later than 2:00 p.m. and these, these need to be taken to Mr. Johnson's office for signature and dropped off to Ms. Wilson's office by 10:45 a.m.." Tineshia has a look of defeat on her face. "You good love?" Stephanie asks.

Tineshia tries to perk up. "yeah, yeah. I'm good. Get signatures and bring these to Ms. Wilson by 10:45 and get these filled out by 2:00. Got it." Stephanie smiles and walks away. Tineshia exhales deeply. She finishes typing, stands up, grabs the files, and heads to the elevator.

She gets off on the top floor.

"Can I help you?" asks the secretary.

"Yes. I have some files for Mr. Johnson." responds Tineshia.

"Some files?" the secretary responds.

"Yes... I was told he had to sign these immediately."

"Do you work here? You must be new. Hold on a second." The secretary goes into Mr. Johnson's office briefly, then opens the door again. "Mr. Johnson is ready for you."

When Tineshia walks in, William is at his desk and an older man is sitting in a chair. "Excuse me, Mr. Johnson." Tineshia says. William looks up, notices her, and smiles, but before he can say anything, the man in the chair stands up.

"Well, which Johnson are you looking for? I hope it's me." He sticks out his hand.

"Please excuse my father, Ms. Wite," William says. "Dad, this is one of our newer interns... Ms. Wite."

Tineshia reaches out to shake William Johnson senior's, 6'0 68 year old white man with an extended belly in a tailored dark grey suit, hand. He lifts her hand and kisses it.

"Well, hello there, Ms. Wite. You can call me Bill or BJ." He winks at her. William, a smile on his face, shakes his head. “How are you liking it here?” asks Bill. “I hope we are treating you well.”

“Dad, the lady has only been here a week or so.” William interjects.

“Well, if anyone ever gives you any problems, please let me know.” says Bill, causing Tineshia to blush.

“Dad, I think she is going to need that hand back. You have some files for me? Bill releases Tineshia’s hand and she walks towards William's desk. William, while reviewing and signing the documents, speaks softly. “I apologize for my father. He falls asleep in our sexual harassment trainings.”

“Well, now I know why you’re so smooth.” Tineshia whispers and smirks.

“I may need to brush up on my smoothness this weekend if you’re free?”

“Well, I do have a lot of work on my plate. My boss is very demanding.” Tineshia grabs the signed files and starts to exit.

“Son who is in our hiring department?" Bill remarks. "They are doing an excellent job finding talent.” says Bill. Tineshia rolls her eyes and closes the office door. “So I heard y’all over there whispering. Is that you, son? Cause I would definitely be having some fun with that.”

"Really, Dad? I'm sure Mom would be happy to know this."

Bill rolls his eyes. "Son, I love your mother, she means the world to me, but I'm just talking about a lil fun. Now, it has been...what, two years since your wife died? I'm not saying you bring someone like that home, but why not have some fun? You know what I mean?"

"Someone like that?" asks William.

Bill sighs loudly. "I know you guys are all inclusive, PC and all now but come on. You not about to bring no black girl home into all we got going on. I mean, come on son."

William shakes his head "I really can't believe you still feel like that, Dad. Especially over the last thirty years. Why are you so adamant on looking down and trying to hold people back? Black, Brown, Asian...like, come on, they are people just like us no more no less."

Bill has a stern look on his face. "Son, I'm not looking down on them, but they don't know what it takes to create something real. Listen to me. I have started introducing you to some real powerful people. They really know what it means to shape and create something. You need to smarten up now, my boy. I'm trying to hand you down something real, a legacy, but you must watch this type of talk." Bill walks out with an attitude.

Tineshia drops the files off at Ms. Wilson's office, then goes to file the remaining documents. It's now 3:05 p.m.; Tineshia is exhausted and sitting at her desk. She notices Stephanie walking towards her. Anticipating more work, she instantly gets annoyed but tries to control her facial expression.

"Were you able to file those documents?" asks Stephanie.

"Yes, I just got back. I didn't even take my lunch today."

"Oh well, I guess you haven't checked your emails yet."

"No, not yet. You mind just telling me, what they need done?"

"No, hon," Stephanie says. "I guess Mr. Bill or one of them just got laid or something, because they actually acknowledged us for our hard work and everything and gave us Friday off. I just told my husband to drop the kids off with the grandparents, you hear me. We about to have a kid free three-day weekend." Tineshia and Stephanie laugh.

While they are talking. Tineshia's phone rings. When she checks it, she sees a message from William. "See you Friday evening. Wear something you don't mind getting wet." And sends a wink emoji. Tineshia blushes.

It's 12:30 pm on Friday, Tineshia is packing a bag in her room when Ty, her 6'1 17 year old sun kissed cousin with a low cut cesar with 360 waves, bursts in. "What's good, cuz?"

Tineshia shakes her head. "Yo, how many times I got to tell you to knock?"

"It's the middle of the day," says Ty. Not like you naked or nothing. Hold up. Where you think you going?"

Tineshia continues moving around the room. "What you mean?"

Ty pulls a piece of clothing out of her bag. "I mean...I don't think you wearing this down the street."

Tineshia snatches it out of his hand and throws it into the bag. "Why ain't you at school?"

"We supposed to be doing our college applications today."

"So, I don't see no papers in your hand. What's going on?"

"Aht, aht. Don't be trying to change the subject." Ty starts counting on his fingers. "You got a new job, but you not at work. We all know you would sleep eighteen hours if you could, but you not resting, and you packing a bag with some outfits. I don't even think you can fit for real." Tineshia punches Ty on the arm. Ty laughs. "So, it seems like my cousin fresh out the pen and now she bout to get out here in these streets, huh. So, who is he?"

"First of all, you, last I checked you ain't my daddy, mother, or big brother, so I don't know who you think you questioning. And B, what is this 'in the streets' mess you and your sister keep talking about? What does that even mean?"

Ty is laughing, "Damn, you been gone a while. 'In the streets' mean you out here, you know what I mean? You showing some skin, being flirtatious, letting people know you available and ready, you know what I'm saying?"

Tineshia wrinkles her face. "Available and ready? Ready for what? Available to who? Y'all just be coming up with anything."

Betty shows up in the doorway. "What's going on in here?"

Tineshia throws her hands up. "The one day I'm off, everybody stay home, huh? Damn, Tye the only one missing from the party in my room."

"My sister went over to her friend's house so they could do they applications together." says Ty.

"You should have went with them." Tineshia says.

"Nah, Tye gets mad cause her friends be thinking I'm cute." Ty pops his collar.

Betty walks further into the room and starts looking around. "And your daddy at work, where I thought you were."

"Oh no, Aunty... T off today."

"I see and she not in the bed sleeping? What's really going on?" Betty notices the bag. "You going somewhere, daughter of mines?"

"I think she got a date, Aunty. She trying to sneak away when she thought nobody was home and all."

"Shut up. TJ." Tineshia says sternly. TJ starts laughing.

Betty walks closer to Tineshia. "Mmm hmm, so where you think you going, T, huh?"

Tineshia says softly, "just out," with her head lowered.

"Out with who? Where y'all going?"

Tineshia's phone pings. She checks it and it's a message from William: "You about ready?"

"More than." Tineshia replies

Betty tries to look over her shoulder, "Hmm, who's that?" Tineshia's phone pings again. William: "B outside in 5."

"Huh? Huh?" Betty asks.

"I got to go." Tineshia grabs her bag and leaves the room quickly. TJ and Betty look at each other and slowly follow. Tineshia opens the front door and walks out. When she tries to close the door, her mother grabs it.

"I got the door, don't worry about it. I want to get some fresh air anyway." Betty says. Ty grinning right behind her.

Tineshia sighs "Y'all are doing the most."

The all-black Mercedes pulls up. Chad steps out and walks around the back of the car. "Good day, Ms. Wite. Are you ready?" he asks

"Oh, so this your date?" says Ty. "I mean, homie car is nice, but he looks jive lame. Hey, my man, have her home early, you understand?"

Tineshia whispers, "Boy, shut the fuck up. That's not him, that's his driver."

"Oh, his driver, huh?" Betty interjects. "Well, you might want to stay out a little later, huh?"

Tineshia rolls her eyes and walks towards the car. "I'm so sorry about that, Chad."

Chad opens the rear passenger door. "Not a problem, no problem at all, Ms. Wite." he closes the door walks back to the driver's door, gets in, and pulls off.

45 minutes later, the car pulls up to a marina, where William is standing outside. Chad gets out, walks around, and opens the door for Tineshia. She gets out and locks eyes with William. He is dressed in all white linen vest and pants. "You're looking quite handsome," remarks Tineshia. I think I'm underdressed." Tineshia has on jean shorts and a sleeveless top.

"No matter what I wear, I would still pale in comparison to you."

Tineshia blushes. "Well I'm definitely about to change."

William takes her hand, and walks her down the dock and onto the boat; where the yacht staff meets them and escorts them on-board. The yacht has 2 levels, 4 cabins, a galley on the main level. On the upper level is the cockpit and deck. The deck features a covered space for entertaining as well as uncovered space for sunbathing.

The boat sets off. Tineshia has now changed into her bathing suit, with a cover up over her legs. She is standing alone on the boat, looking at the water, when a member of staff brings her a glass of wine. She turns and notices William staring at her. "How long have you been there?" she asks.

"Time has seemed to stand still." William says. "I really have no idea."

"You and your dad just always say the right thing, huh?"

William scoffs "My dad."

"What you mean?"

"My dad...hmm how to put it? He is from what seems like an ancient time. He doesn't respect or even seem to see the progress we as a society have made over the last fifty years."

"Oh." Tineshia stands silent, not sure what to say.

"He isn't a bad guy. I guess he's just set in his ways, you know what I mean?"

"Well, when you've made it rich and own your own firm, I guess nobody can tell you nothing."

"Yeah, but with great power should come great

responsibility. But far too often that's not the case." Tineshia raises her eyebrows and sips her wine. "Anyway, how you enjoying the firm?"

"I like it." Tineshia says. "It's hard work, but I'm learning a lot about the law in ways I don't think I would have on my own...and they not teaching us in class, that's for sure."

"I been hearing good things. Some who had questions are very impressed with your work ethic."

Tineshia smiles and slowly strolls away from William before looking back. "So, you been checking on me? Spying on me?" She turns around and starts walking backwards now, one step at a time.

William smiles and starts slowly walking towards her. "As I told you in the beginning, I am in awe of you. I think you're inspiring, and I wanted to see if you inspired others."

Tineshia keeps walking backwards step by step. "So, seems it's about time I talk to my boss about a raise right, since I'm inspiring others?" She backs up against a wall and can't back up any further.

William continues to slowly walk up, and is now face to face with Tineshia. He whispers, "Oh, really?" He leans in and kisses her. "And about that raise." He takes her hand, while kissing her again, and slowly guides her hand to his groin.

Tineshia smiles. “That’s a good starting point.” She kisses him. “I think we can negotiate.” William kisses her aggressively and passionately. He picks her up while they are kissing and takes her inside.

At this time, what neither of them...hovering over the boat there is a drone taking pictures. A women on shore is controlling the drone and recording.

The boat pulls back up to the docks. Tineshia is getting dressed. “I hope your driver don’t mind getting a speeding ticket,” she says. “I’m going to need him to break the speed barrier for me not to miss curfew. I totally lost track of time.” William is smiling, while Tineshia is frantically trying to get all her stuff together. She looks at him noticing the look on his face. “Did I say something funny? I’m going to have to call one of the lawyers at the firm if they violate me for missing curfew.”

William stands up and walks to a desk in the room. “Well, they rarely violate someone for missing curfew one time, so I think you would have a good case.” He opens the desk and pulls out a letter. “I have something for you” he walks toward Tineshia.

“What’s this?” He hands her the letter. She opens it and sits down.

The letter states she has been a model parolee, and since she has shown herself able to reintegrate into society, they are ending her parole and she is now free.

"What..? How...?" Tineshia stammers and starts to cry.

William sits down next to her. "With power, comes responsibility. So, I made a few calls." Tineshia kisses and hugs him.

"Hold on, what are we doing here?" She holds up the letter. "Is this real?"

"It's either very real or a great forgery. That watermark and seal is extremely hard to fake. As for what are we doing, I won't speak for you, but I am not just running game on you. I told you I'm proud of you, I'm in awe of you, and you are inspiring. Now, those words would just be hollow if, I didn't try to do what I could to make sure someone with those attributes wasn't free to make the most of their potential."

"But why me?" Tineshia asks.

William leans in and whispers. "Why not you?" he kisses Tineshia softly.

"Hold up, William, you know I'm not blind, right?" asks Tineshia.

"What do you mean?" Williams asks confused.

Tineshia grabs his left hand, "What about this William? You said no games, right? What about your wife? Are you trying to make me a mistress or something?"

William stands up and slowly walks away "I thought the word would have gotten to you at the office. No, I'm not trying to make you a mistress. My wife died two years ago of breast cancer."

Tineshia stands up and moves towards him. "No. No one told me, I had no idea, I'm so sorry."

"I know this is new, but I would hope you wouldn't think I was that type of guy."

"Listen, I'm really sorry. I saw the ring and didn't know what to think. I haven't been out of prison a whole year, and out of nowhere, this handsome, wealthy guy just starts talking to me, and next thing I know, I have a job and am taking boat trips. I mean, things like that just don't happen in my world."

"That's the problem," William says. "It happens every day in mine."

"Hmm, so you telling me, Mr. Johnson, you going to change my world?"

"Yours to start." They feel the boat stop. "We're back. I guess we need to get you back home."

"I'm not in a rush. I'm a free woman now." Tineshia passionately kisses William.

"Well, how about we get this off your ankle? I have a guy meeting us at the marina."

As William and Tineshia are walking off the boat. A woman with a telephoto lens takes pictures of Tineshia as she meets with the tech. The guy bends down and takes her ankle monitor off. The women takes still photos of the whole thing, as well as of Tineshia kissing William as he helps her into the car. After the car has pulled off, the women packs up her drone, the camera and drives away.

As Tineshia pulls up at home, both her parents are standing on the porch. She checks her phone and notices it is dead. "Shit."

"Is everything okay, Ms. Wite?" asks Chad

"I didn't realize my phone was off. I know my family ready to cuss me out. They must have been worried sick because of the time."

"Well, I think their feelings may change with the information you have for them."

"Yeah...after my mother kills me, she may bring me back to life."

As Chad gets out of the car. John starts walking down from the porch angrily. "Sir what is your name? I don't care who the fuck you work for. Who y'all think y'all are, having my daughter miss curfew? What are y'all trying to do."

Tineshia sees her father and his attitude and knows she cannot afford to wait for Chad to open her door. He might not make it. She opens the car door herself. Chad is at the trunk with his hands up. Tineshia jumps out. "Daddy, Daddy. It's okay, it's okay. Chad it is ok, thank you. Chad starts backing up. "Okay, Ms. Wite. Have a good evening."

"Daddy, listen. Everything is okay."

Betty chimes in. "T, we have been calling your phone like crazy, Where the hell you been?"

"Baby, you're so close to being done with all this. Why would you jeopardize everything?" says John.

"Mom, Dad, stop, stop please let me explain. I'm so sorry I worried y'all. My phone died and I didn't notice."

"Did your watch die too?" Betty interrupts. "We need to get in the house. Them people about to start calling soon wondering why you missed curfew, or do they just pull up? We going to have to come up with a good one for this. Alright, listen... you were out with one of the twins and they fell sick, and you had to take them to the E.R. Let me call Tye so she knows to go check in at the hospital."

"The monitors have GPS that wouldn't... listen, mom don't call Tye, okay? Everything is ok." Tineshia shows her ankle.

"T what the hell have you done?" exclaims John. "You know these things have sensors or tracker or something on it and you going to straight to jail for this. Are you on something? Did they drug you or something?"

Tineshia reaches into her purse and pulls out the letter. "Daddy no, look." She hands the letter to her father.

"Shit, what is that?" asks Betty. She walks quickly off the porch towards John.

"I am free!" screams Tineshia. "Totally, absolutely, one hundred percent free." John hands the letter to Betty. "Daddy, I'm free!"

John smiles and hugs her. "You're free. It's over." Tineshia and John spin while they hug.

"I'm free!"

"But how?" Betty asks while reading the letter, puzzled. "I thought you still had a few months left."

Tineshia thinks for a good way to respond. "I guess my firm sent them a request or something since I been killing it there. I don't know. I don't care. I'm free, Mommy." Betty hugs Tineshia and John.

CHAPTER 8

BACKGROUND CHECK

William gets a call on his way home.

"Son, we need to talk. Can you come by the house?" asks Bill

"Yeah, I can. Is everything okay?" William responds

"Your mother and I need to talk to you as soon as you can."

"Okay. I'll be there shortly." William speaks to his driver. "Chad, we need to make a stop by my parents' house."

Chad looks through the rearview mirror. "Yes, sir."

William arrives at his parents' house, when he enters,

he is greeted by his mother, 5'6 blond haired 40C 150lb white Elizabeth (Lizzy) and Bill. Bill has an envelope in his hand. William II says, a look of concern on his face, "Is everything okay? What's wrong?"

"Son, come with us." says Bill

William follows him into the other room and all three take a seat. "I know we were just shooting the shit the other day in your office, but is there something going on with you and the new intern?"

"Excuse me?" William asks confused

"Son, we understand you're still hurting from the loss of Christine." says Lizzy. "You're a man and need to let off some steam."

"Mom!"

"We understand if you want to have some fun and all, if that's what this is." says Bill

"If what is what?" William stands up. "I'm not doing this, not having this conversation, and I am not listening to this. I'm grown; I don't have to explain myself."

Bill slides the envelope towards him. "It's not us asking."

"What's this?" William opens the envelope. Out pours a stack of pictures and papers. He sits back down. "Y'all are having me followed?" he says in disbelief.

"No, son." says Lizzy

"No. Listen...I told you, you're being vetted." says Bill

William looks over all the photos and papers. "What the hell?"

"This is no joke," Bill says. "This is serious business. This is not just a credit check. This vetting includes who you keep company with."

"What does she have to do with it?" asks William

"Nothing, nothing at all. Look; you want to have some fun, that is fine." says Bill

"Some fun? What does that even mean? Why does it matter to anyone who I date?" asks William

"Date?" interjects Lizzy. "You are trying to date her?"

"And what if I am, Mom?"

Lizzy and Bill look at each other. Lizzy puts her head down and shakes her head..

"Son; I understand you have some progressive thoughts..." remarks Bill

"Progressive? Is this because she's black? Y'all cannot be serious!" exclaims William

"Willy," his mother says," you can do so much better."

"I really hate it when you call me that, and I really hate that y'all still have these views." says William

"Bill, tell him. These people can't be trusted." Lizzy says to Bill

"*These people*? Mom, you really need to get your closet racism under control. If you got to know her, you would know just how beautiful and resilient her spirit is."

Lizzy rolls her eyes. "I am far from racist. I have plenty of black friends."

"Really, Mom? What, you got two friends of color who don't work for you?"

"You forgot about Jocelyn. Her father is from South Africa."

William snickers. "He is an old white South African. Mom. You don't know about apartheid?"

"Listen, son." Bill says. "You don't seem to fully understand. We are trying to introduce you to a society that will continue our family legacy. You will be connected in ways you cannot fully understand. You will be instrumental in preserving and shaping the global future, do you understand? I don't think you fully grasp the gravity and complexity of what we are a part of."

"Yeah, I hear you. Dad, but what does Ms. Wite have to do with that?"

"You have to show you're fully committed. Your associations and the company you keep speaks to the character of who you are."

"Ms. Wite would be an excellence character reference."

Bill picks up one of the files. "A 23-year-old ex-con with a GED, convicted for aggravated assault and attempted robbery. Parents: Betty is currently a social worker, who couldn't keep her own daughter out of jail and who also has a record. Let's see___, ah yes, she pled guilty to shoplifting and a sub 600 credit score. As well as Mr. John Wite. Construction worker___, excuse me, foreman___, multiple assault and battery charges... I guess she's just a chip off the old block, huh. And let us not miss that, he's currently over extended with a second mortgage and no equity in his home. This is your rave reference?"

"Just because someone isn't good on paper doesn't

make them a bad person Dad. She is sweet, resilient, hard-working, smart. You know she got her degree while she was in jail, only one year behind the people she went to school with?

"Listen. Where you're headed, she cannot go. Period." Bill exclaims. "This is an exclusive membership that has been cultivated in our family dating back to last century, and there are rules. I am sick, son." Lizzy grabs Bill's hand. "We have other people that want our family spot. I have to get you caught up and caught up quickly."

William has a look of concern on his face. "Dad."

"It's okay. They say I have two years__ maybe three."

William hugs Bill. Bill grabs William firmly behind his neck. "You need to take this seriously. I need you to take this seriously. It's going to be your responsibility to take care of your mom and safeguard our family legacy." William, with tears in his eyes, stares into his father's eyes.

William walks out the door of his parents' house and towards his car. Bill and Lizzy wave to him as Chad closes the car door and gets in to drive away. After the car has gone, Bill closes the house door.

"Billy, he is not ready." Lizzy says.

"Well, he's going to have to get there."

"Or you can just go to the group and tell them you're going to have me temporarily fill in until he's ready."

Bill rolls his eyes. "Honey, you already know. I didn't make the rules, but they are not letting any more women in right now after the last incident."

"But they have let women in the group before. You told me how hard you had to fight to get her in. It's not like I'm a black person or something." Lizzy pleads.

"Elizabeth, the women that have been part of the group were allowed in because there were no male heirs available. Since I was the one who pushed that situation, I can't be the one to do it again. William may be a little naïve, but we're going to have to get him up to snuff. And you are going to have to accept your place. If we don't want to lose our place and position, William has to be the one."

CHAPTER 9

TOO GOOD TO BE TRUE

Tineshia is at her desk typing on the computer. Stephanie comes over. "I am so happy the day is damn near over can't believe it's only Wednesday, though."

"I know, right?" Tineshia agrees. "This week does seem to be dragging, but I can't wait to get out of here. I have a couple of apartments to look at."

"Aww, shit now. You and your secret boo finally going to go public and get a place together?" asks Stephanie

Tineshia smiles. "There is no boo, secret or otherwise. Just think it's about time to get my own place, that's all."

"Uh huh, it's cool, you don't want to tell me yet... it's cool. Listen, before you start your apartment hunt, I need you to take these up to Mr. Johnson's office before you get out of here, --- thank you. Hey, maybe let him know you looking for an apartment. I think he has a few real estate contacts."

Tineshia smirks as Stephanie walks away, then she gets up and walks towards the elevator. She gets into the elevator and presses the "up" button. As the elevator is going up, Tineshia is smiling, happy about to see her "secret boo." After getting off the elevator on the executive floor, she walks towards William's office and notices his secretary appears to have already left for the day. As she gets closer to the office, the door opens. Out of the office comes Bill.

"Ms. Wite, how are you today?" asks Bill

"I'm good sir, thank you." Tineshia responds

Bill corrects her. "Please, no 'sir', BJ, remember?"

"Yes, yes, that's right---, just a level of respect I was raised with."

"I understand," says Bill. "Manners are often lost on people, so I totally understand. It is a good thing when one knows their place. Have a good evening. Ms. Wite." He pats Tineshia on the shoulder as he walks away. Tineshia looks after him, confused and upset. She knocks on William's door.

"Come in." William yells

Tineshia walks in. "Hey, I just saw your father and... umm..."

William rolls his eyes. "Oh my goodness, what did the old man do now?"

"Your dad ... he just made a comment referencing me knowing my place."

William gets up and goes to close the door. "So, we need to talk."

Tineshia crosses her arms and looks at William shockingly. "Oh, yeah. I guess we do. What the hell was that about?"

"Yeah, so, people know about us." says William

"People? Who are people? You mean your parents? It's been like a handful of dates. What is there to know?" asks Tineshia

William faking a look of hurt on his face. "I mean shit, make a man feel special, why don't you. Just a hand full of dates, huh"

Tineshia rolls her eyes. "You know what I mean."

"I'm just playing. Please have a seat." Tineshia sits down. "So, I met you at a remarkably interesting point. Let's see ... how to even begin this?"

"William, listen. Just be upfront with me, okay? If there's a problem, just say it." Tineshia sighs anticipating a 'shoe to drop'.

"No, T, it's not you---, nothing you did. Fuck it, look, I trust you, okay? Everything I am about to tell you must stay between me and you, do you understand? This is not a game. This could put a lot of people's lives in danger, okay?"

Tineshia sits up in the chair. "Shit, am I in danger? What's going on?"

William sits on his desk, "Everything people think or have been made to think is a conspiracy is real. There is a very exclusive group of white mostly men, with a few women, that have been behind and responsible for designing and guiding this country since its inception."

Tineshia frowns. "So you're saying there is some secret cabal or something?"

"This is not a joke." William gets up, walks around his desk, opens a drawer, and pulls out a folder. He passes the folder across the desk and sits down. "I need you to really understand this." Tineshia stands up and leans on the desk.

"What is this?" She opens the envelope and pulls out the file. Tineshia looks at the files with concern. "You had someone do background on me? Hold up--- this has my mom and dad in here too? My cousins...William, what the fuck is this?"

"I didn't do this." exclaims William. "If you look in the folder, it also has pictures from this weekend." Tineshia pours out the remaining contents of the folder. "After our date, on my way home. I got called to my parents' house and presented with this. My father told me a few months ago he had submitted me for acceptance to some society and that it was my legacy or some shit. I thought it was just another country club, yacht club thing."

Tineshia is still looking through the paperwork. "What this got to do with me and my family?"

"They're vetting me, and that includes any and everyone that is, or they see as, or could be part of my world to see if I'm worthy to join. You see, my father is sick, and since I'm the only male heir, our legacy seat is on me."

"So, you're telling me, because I'm in your orbit, me and my whole family is under investigation? Is that why your father is telling me about my place?

"T, this is an incredibly old society with incredibly old rules, and like I said at the beginning, all the members, whether men or women, are white. Apparently, they only started allowing women of families who had no male heir under specific circumstances recently."

"Un huh. So, women are allowed, but black people aren't. I still don't understand what this got to do with me and my family. It's not like I'm applying to this society."

William stands up and walks to Tineshia and takes her hand. "You don't understand. I don't even know how long they've been following me, but what they are saying here is that they are seeing you and me as a potential real thing, otherwise they wouldn't be dedicating all these resources."

Tineshia pulls her hand away. "I don't know. Will. I mean. I just don't know. This is a lot. I like you; I really like you, but what are you talking about here? We got people doing research on me, my parents, my whole damn family. Your family may have signed up for this shit, but mine did not. Then what? You want to put your whole family's legacy on the line to be with me? Already your father saying I need to go back in my place. And you want to challenge some ancient society over me? I'm not your wife---, shit, we haven't had any conversations about what we actually are."

"T. I know it's a lot, but understand this. I'm not going to let anyone dictate to me who I am or am not going to be with." William's office phone starts ringing. He talks over the noise while walking to answer it. "Hello? Yes. Ms. Wite came by my office and brought me the paperwork. We are having a discussion now. Yes. thank you. Aight, bye." He hangs up. Stephanie was just checking up on you."

"I bet; it's been a minute." Tineshia replies

William smiles. “Well, hey, it’s nice when you have friends with connections.”

“Friends, huh? Is that what we are?” William’s face straightens. “Can you approve me going home early, friend? This is a lot to process, I can’t think right now.”

William walks around to Tineshia and grabs her hand. “Listen, I know this is a lot, but I’m not backing down for these guys, and I like you T. I need you to know that.” Tineshia puts her head down. William lifts her chin. “Never drop your head. You are equal to the best of them out there and better than most of them, you hear me?” He leans in and kisses her.

She looks into his eyes, and whispers. “I got to go.” She pulls away and walks out. William bangs on the desk.

Tineshia looks back at the office door after she hears a bang come from it. As she exits the building, she pulls out her phone and calls Zahra, “Hey Z, y’all busy? Girl, I don’t know what I done got myself into. Yeah, I’m on the way.”

CHAPTER 10

IT'S NOT PARANOIA WHEN...

Tineshia walks into the coffee shop. “Hey, Marci, how you been? Tell Zahra I’m in the back, okay?” As she is walking towards her table, a 5' 10 expresso complected 42D 240lb slim waisted black lady, seemingly distracted by her phone, bumps into her and spills her coffee.

“I’m so sorry.” she says.

“It’s okay. No harm, no foul. The coffee spilled on the floor, not on me.” Tineshia responds

“It was totally my fault. Please let me buy your coffee.” The lady says embarrassed

“It’s all good--- really. I used to work here, matter of fact." Tineshia turns to the front counter. "Marci.... can we get her another one and I'll take my usual?" Marci nods in agreement.

The woman looks Tineshia up and down, "You used to work here? I would have never guessed from the way you are dressed." Tineshia has on a mustard colored blazer and pants with a white shirt and black heels. "Damn, girl. Talk about a come up." Tineshia blushes. "Not to be too formal, but I bumped into you and you got me a coffee? You have to allow me a chance to repay the kindness. Let me take you out for dinner and you can explain to me your road to greatness."

"Thank you, but I have a boyfriend...or something. Anyway, it's really nothing. Most people cause an accident, then try and blame the other person. It's refreshing to meet someone with manners."

"Hold up. Let's circle back to this, 'or something'? Because, honey, someone like you shouldn't be wasting your time on someone who has you guessing."

Zahra comes out the back, carrying three cups of coffee. "Hey. T, you made a new friend." She hands the woman her order.

"Yeah, I kinda just bumped into her." Tineshia says.

The woman takes the coffee from Zahra. "Thank you--- T, is it?" She hands Tineshia her card. "Think about it, eh?" She winks at Tineshia as she caresses the back of her arm, discreetly placing a listening device on her sleeve. She turns away, puts in a Bluetooth earbud, and walks towards her table.

Zahra snickers and whispers, "Think about it."

Tineshia rolls her eyes at Zahra. "Shut up. Listen, after the day I've had, I just might."

Zahra raises her eyebrows. "Oh really? So your time away wasn't all bad, huh?"

"Fuck you, huh." Tineshia and Zahra laugh as they walk towards their table.

As they sit down, Zahra says "So, what's up girl? What have you gotten into now with your cushy job and that super-hot boyfriend?"

"Z, girl!", Tineshia looks around the café and leans in. "This is some next level shit."

Zahra laughs. "What you mean? He asked you to marry him or something? And why you looking around and whispering? What, you a spy now? The CIA recruiting you now?"

"Z, this is serious--- some people following me type of shit."

“Following you? Like what--- some type of background check or something?”

“No, Z, just listen." Tineshia starts explaining. "I’m headed to William’s office to get his signature, right?”

“Mm_hmm, his signature. That’s what y’all calling it? Zahra interrupts

Tinisha, getting frustrated, rolls her eyes. “Z, do you want to hear or not? This is not a joke.”

“I’m sorry, I’m sorry, please.”

“So I get to his office and his dad comes out, sees me, and makes this comment like it’s good that I know my place.”

“Your place?” Zahra says. “Nah, fuck that. Who he think he is?”

“Right, so I go into the office to ask Will what’s that about. He drops this envelope on me, has pictures of Will and me, as well as a report and pictures of my mom, dad, cousins, and details of their past. I’m talking about my parents’ credit report, criminal records, who they were talking to prior to being married, voting record.”

Zahra leans in. “What the fuck?”

“Yeah, that’s how I was. So apparently Will’s father is

connected to some type of cabal or something and Will's the heir. Because of that, they're watching and vetting him. They caught on to us, so they're vetting me as well."

"Hold up, back up--- what you mean, a cabal?" Zahra asks confused

"All I know is, it's some super-secret group of predominantly men, white men at that, and they are not too excited that their possible new member is dating a black girl."

Zahra sits back in her chair. "But who are these people?"

Unbeknownst to them, the woman, drinking her coffee, is listening intently.

"Girl. I don't know. All he told me is it's some real powerful old society." Tineshia shrugs.

Zahra looks around the café and leans in. "So are they watching me?"

"You weren't in the files Will showed me, but I don't know what this is."

"So, are you going to tell your parents? You going to keep seeing Will? Like, what you going to do, T?"

"I don't know. Z! What would you do? I mean, Will

say this is only happening because he really likes me and they can tell. I mean, I do like him, but what am I supposed to do with this racist old boys' club following me and my peoples?"

Zahra sips her coffee. "What did Will say?"

"He said how much he likes me and he's not going to let them tell him what to do and this and that, but *girl!* We only been talking like a few months, you know? Shit, I ain't even met his family and they already don't like me and telling me to stay in my place and shit. I don't know what to do."

"Shit, I say you at least stick around so you can find out who these people are and expose these racist assholes. Fuck them, you feel me? Fuck that job. You can come back and work here. You don't need Will or his family; you got family right here."

Tineshia stands up, walks around the table, and hugs Zahra.

Discreetly, the woman takes a picture with her phone and starts to pack up.

While they're hugging. Zahra notices her standing up, "Uh oh, I think your girlfriend mad you hugging me." Tineshia releases and looks over.

The woman blows a kiss towards Tineshia and mouths "call me!" as she picks up her stuff and leaves.

Zahra "see if things don't work out with Will, you already got your next one lined up." Zahra and Tineshia laugh.

CHAPTER 11

THE ORGANIZATION

It is 2:52 p.m. Bill (who controls Maine, New Hampshire, Vermont, Massachusetts, Rhode Island, Connecticut, New York, New Jersey, Delaware, District of Columbia, Maryland, and Virginia), Matthew, 45 year old 5'8 190lb white man from Colorado with brown hair and a full beard (who controls Idaho, Montana, Wyoming, North Dakota, South Dakota, Nebraska, Colorado and Utah), Curt a 57 year old 6'0 250lb tan cleanly shaven white man from California (who controls Washington, Oregon, Nevada, California, Arizona, and New Mexico), James a 62 year old 5'7 215lb pale white man with a goatee and glasses from West Virginia (who controls West Virginia, Kentucky, Tennessee, North Carolina and South Carolina), and Tiffany a 42 year old 5'6 185lb white woman with greyish blonde hair and glasses from Michigan (who controls Pennsylvania, Ohio, Indiana, Illinois, Wisconsin, and Michigan) are sitting at a round table in a boardroom having a conversation.

In walks Steve a 65 year old 5'8 175lb white man with low cut white hair from Texas (who controls Texas, Oklahoma, Kansas, Arkansas, Louisiana, Mississippi, Alabama, Georgia, and Florida) . "Good afternoon, lady and gentlemen." he says in a strong southern drawl. Everyone becomes quiet.

"Nice of you to join us." Bill says. "See you still moving at a nice southern pace. We agreed on 2:30 p.m. , didn't we?"

Steve chuckles. "Well, hell it's only 1:52 in Texas, so, I would actually have been early if you'd come to me. Since you and yours are the reason we're having this emergency meeting I don't even understand why we had to come to you in the first place."

"Fellas, come on, this is no way to start." Tiffany says. "We're all on the same side and want the same things."

"Mrs. Bennett," says Steve. "Big Bill's defender right on cue. How are you, honey? Bill, I know I wasn't the only one here who thought there was, let us say, ulterior motives." He winks at Tiffany. "When you fought so hard to have Tiffany as our first female member. But, she has proven to be one of our best, and skilled at handling things diplomatically."

"You come twenty minutes late and within the first five minutes challenge and degrade one of our members?" Bill shakes his head.

"Degrade? I said she is very, very skilled." Steve looks Tiffany up and down and sucks his teeth. "Our Tiffany came up in Michigan. She is tough. You aren't offended, are you, honey?"

"Not at all, Mr. Richards. Ford wasn't the only thing made tough in Michigan. And I truly am appreciative to be the latest, youngest, and first female member of our organization. Bill, we should cut Steve some slack. We understand Steve is our most senior member and sometimes it's harder for him to be able to, uh, *get up* like he used to." Matthew, Curt, James, and Bill snicker.

"That was cute, honey." Steve says. "Can we get this meeting started?"

"Okay." James cuts in. "We have called this emergency meeting due to clause 5 of our charter---, member health concerns. Specifically, William Johnson and his succession plan."

Bill stands up. "Yes, In keeping with our founding charter, at our last annual meeting. I disclosed that I have been given a terminal diagnosis by our physician. I have been given three to five years projected time frame. I have already started and will continue to prepare my son William Johnson II to be my successor, as is our tradition."

"Your son," Steve asks. "Are you sure he understands

our history and can be a positive contributor for us? He is a little young."

"My son has graduated from Harvard and has been successfully running the biggest firm on the east coast, fostering and developing his own relationships with influential leaders, and will continue to add to this organization, as all Johnsons have from the start."

"Yes." Steve knocks on the glass. In walks a woman with a briefcase, the same woman who was watching Tineshia and Zahra in the café. "Thank you. Felicia" She exits. "Your son's relationships and who is influencing who is what concerns me." Steve puts the briefcase on the table and opens it. He begins to pass out files to the other members. "In your packets you will see information on the people young William chooses to associate with and, their views, not to mention criminal records. Now, although Mrs. Bennett is our latest and youngest member, her family is one of the founding families. Now when Bob died, tragically and unexpectedly, as an organization, we vetted Bob's son Zach. Curt and I believed, that with our knowledge and experience, we could mold Zach and he should be his family's rightful successor." Steve shrugs. "But we were out-voted by Bill, James, and Tiffany's father Michael may he rest in peace. Now, the reason that you yourself gave, Bill, was that Zach associated with people whose agenda did not line up with our own. You even used his wife being Latina, as a reason we couldn't expect him to fall in line. On the basis of this, how can we trust your son?

James is reading through his file "Your son is serious... like seriously dating a colored woman?"

"Unlike in the case of Bob's tragedy," Bill says. "I have time to teach my son our history and the importance of what we do. And yes, Steve brought his concerns and files to me a few weeks ago and I have already addressed them with my son. James, everyone, we all know how hard it has been on my son since his wife died. He has assured me that this is a merely an infatuation with this woman--- I believe it to be more of a charity case than anything else."

Tiffany raises her eyes from reading to look at Bill with disappointment.

Steve stands up, walks to the door, and knocks on the glass, "He has assured you, has he?" Felicia walks in again and hands Steve a laptop, then walks out. Steve opens the computer, pulls out a speaker from his briefcase, and turns the computer to the other members. "Once Bill informed us of his diagnosis and his desire to have his son take his place at our, table of course, as a descendant of one of the original families I started to vet young William. As he is also one of the last of the three founding family's bloodlines, as a courtesy, a few weeks ago I sent the files you are all reading now to Bill directly. Bill also told me that he, along with his lovely wife Lizzy, were going to straighten things out. Two days ago, my investigator recorded this."

Steve hits play on the laptop. It is a five-minute video

recording of William and Tineshia's conversation in William's office. After the video ends, Matthew and James murmur under their breath. Curt and Tiffany look at each other, then look at Bill. Steve delves into his briefcase and pulls out a recording device. "Your son has chosen to disclose information to someone who has not been vetted or accepted by the group. They shouldn't even know that we even exist. Yet, you say this is a mere infatuation? You say you can get him up to speed, but what I'm hearing is, and I quote, 'I won't let anyone tell me what to do?' This was after you and your wife had already talked to him, right?"

The room goes quiet, with everyone looking at Bill. Bill stands up, "I would like to thank Steve for being proactive and diligent. You didn't have to give me a preview of what was going on in my own house, but you did. As I stated at the beginning, yes, I have been given a terminal diagnosis, and my family and I are just starting to come to grips with this, but I have some time---not much, but I encourage Steven to continue to do his due diligence. I do not expect our organization to show any favoritism towards myself or William; that is not our way. With the time I have left, I will focus on getting my son ready to be a productive member of our organization and preparing all the files so that if the group does not approve of his succession, they will be ready for the next member."

Steve stands walks towards Bill and extends his hand to shake. "I believe I speak for everyone when I say news of your diagnosis rocked us all. You and your family have been instrumental in creating this organization and the whole

United States--- hell, the world would be a lot worse off if not for your steady hand and guidance. I know you will make the most of the time you have left, and if you say young William will be ready, well, hell's bells, that's enough for me."

Curt, Matthew, Tiffany, and James all clap. While shaking hands, Bill pulls Steve in for an embrace. While hugging, Bill whispers. "We need to talk."

Steve responds "our normal spot at 8." They release their embrace smiling.

CHAPTER 12

A TRIP DOWN MEMORY LANE

Bill's car pulls up to a building with no name on it. There is a well-dressed white man pleading with the door man to enter the building. "Sir, there is nothing going on inside." Says the doorman. This place is not open yet."

"Don't try and play me man, look." The guy pulls out $10,000, still wrapped in the band from the bank. "I got money; I know what this place is. Matter of fact, --- here, how bout you take $500, you know? Go ahead and buzz me in or whatever and we all good."

"Keep your money, sir. There is nothing going on." says the doorman

"Yeah, there's nothing going on? Then why are you here?" the man asks

"Sir, I'm going to have to ask you to leave. I don't want to have to call the police."

Ray, a 6'5 275lb muscular bald headed white man in a black suit and black tee-shirt, gets out of the car and walks to the rear passenger door.

"Sir," the doorman says. "you cannot park your car here." Ray ignores him and continues. "I don't know what is going on with people tonight?" The doorman says while looking up to the sky. He walks up to Ray and grabs his shoulder. "Hey, buddy? Are you deaf?" Ray opens the car door and the doorman sees Bill in the backseat. "Oh, sorry, sir. I didn't know it was you." Ray knocks the doorman's hand off his shoulder. "Excuse me. My apologies." Bill steps out of the car and walks into the building. Ray gives the doorman a look and follows Bill inside.

"I thought nothing was going on inside? Who was that old guy?" the man protests.

"I'm not going to tell you again, sir. Move on or I'm calling the police."

Bill walks into the building, followed by Ray. On his left, there is a stage on where an exotic dancer is dancing surrounded by tables with men getting individual dances. On his right, separated from them by clear soundproof glass and a hallway, there are high-stakes casino and card games being played.

Bill and Ray continue to walk down the hallway. They reach an elevator next to a set of steps guarded by security. The guard sees Bill approaching removes the rope and scans his keycard to open the elevator doors. Bill and Ray enter the elevator. When they exit, they are greeted by the concierge and taken into the private area.

"Welcome back, Mr. Johnson." the concierge says. "Mr. Richards has already arrived and is being entertained. Would you like entertainment tonight as well?" A woman in a short red latex dress walks past them with a man on a chain leash.

"No." Bill says. "I will not be needing any entertainment tonight, but who is the guy outside?"

"That's Tim. Was there an issue?" asks the concierge

"Has there been a change to our training program? Seemed like he was ineffectively dealing with a guy outside. He also put his hands on Ray. Are we no longer going through the cars and people who are to be treated as VIPs? asks Bill

The concierge frowns her face. "No, sir. I will address this immediately. And my apologies, Ray.

"No need, darling." Ray winks at the concierge.

They arrive at a back office. The concierge knocks

twice on the door. "You gentlemen have a good evening." She looks at Ray. "And please, if there is any way I can be of assistance, don't hesitate to let me know." The concierge walks away, Ray staring after her.

Bill opens the door. Steve is sitting in a chair with a cigar and a drink, with a black woman in lingerie sitting on his lap, laughing. The music from the exotic room is playing through the speakers. Steve yells, *"Bill!* Come join us. Serita here... did you know this beautiful young thing is in law school? Darling, see, Bill here knows a thing or two about law firms, don't you now, Bill?"

"Ray, you can wait out here?" Bill says

"Absolutely, sir."

"Hey, Serita," Bill continues. "Can you please give me and this southern gentleman a few moments?" He walks over to the wall and turns off the speaker.

"Yes, honey," Steve says. The men have to talk a little business. Don't get lost, though, I want to hear so much more." Serita kisses Steve on the cheek and stands up. Steve smacks her ass, and she walks out of the office, Ray closes the door.

"Mmm mmm mmm," remarks Steve. "I understand how your son could get so mesmerized by them. It's just something about their skin and how it glistens."

"What the fuck, Steve?" Bill says.

"Straight to business, I see." Steve puts down his drink and cigar. "I told you, didn't I? Our families have been through a lot over the years, but at the end of the day, us, your family and mine more than any other, have been the guiding light for this country. But you betrayed all of that."

"Steve, you are still on this? We had one little disagreement---, one! And you going to attack my son, my whole family?"

Steve stands up quickly. "It was not just one little disagreement! You should know after all this time how important our word is, Bill. You made me out to be a liar."

"No matter how you feel about Tiffany, she has been very good for the organization. She has more than earned her place with the work she has done in Indiana and Illinois alone."

Steve shakes his head. "Bill, Bill, Bill. The end does not always justify the means, and you're trying to gloss over the real issue here. Or have you forgotten about Bob?" Bill lowers his head and turns his back to Steve. "Ah yes, so you haven't forgotten."

"Bob was unstable at the end. Steve! He was not respecting our traditions, and he waited too late to start the transition of power to his son. At the end, he was spewing all types of nonsense to his son."

"It was the nature of his disease, Bill. Maybe if we'd had as good a physician as we do now, his dementia could have been diagnosed earlier, like your condition was."

Bill whips around. "Cancer is not the same as dementia!"

"Bill, you and Bob's little feud was not a secret. And Bill...come on...I know you. Everybody else might believe the dementia led to his apparent suicide, but not me. But even though you two were at odds, he was my friend. Early after his diagnosis, he was lucid, and he made me promise that I would help guide his son Zach and look after his family. I came to you! I came to you, Bill, and asked you to vote with me to transfer power to Zach. I never asked you or pressed you about the details of Bobs death. You already had your revenge. But you just had to let your hatred for Bob blind you to everything else. I saw the look on your face when the vote went against Zach. You took pleasure in it. A final fuck you to him beyond his grave. What you could not see through your hatred was that you hurt me too. How could I look his family in the eye after he passed? His wife...I swear she died so quickly afterwards due to shock and disappointment." Bill sits down. "The worst of it is, young Zach turned on his wife, the mother of his children, because of you! You, Bill, made the lynch pin of your case against them about her Latina heritage and obscure family."

"I don't know where you got this idea of me having something to do with Bob's death. Anyway that was over two decades ago, Steve." Bill points at Steve. "And I wasn't the only one who voted against Zach."

"Bill please." Steve raises his hands. "It's me ok. It's me." He puts his hands down. "Don't insult my intelligence ok. Just don't. Time doesn't change the facts. You went to great pains to hijack that vote. You knew James had a bias against Latinos and you played on that. Curt does whatever you say, and it took me a while, but it became evident how you bought Tom Tiffany's father's vote. Nine years ago, I gave you a chance to make it right. I tried to keep Zach close, and when Tom was passing with no male heir, I lobbied you to bring Zach back into the fold. But no, you couldn't do that, could you? No, because you had given your word to Tom. Since he couldn't have a son, you fought hard to make his daughter our first female member. You couldn't go back on your word, huh? What about my word, Bill?"

"What do you want from me? You want me to say, I'm sorry? I went too far. I'm sorry Steve. What do you want from me? I have just been forced to face my own mortality. My family and I have given our lives to this organization. William has an impeccable record---, the best schools, head of one of the biggest and most powerful law firms in the north-east---and he'll be an excellent asset to the organization."

Steve starts to laugh and walks back to his seat. He sits

down and relights his cigar. "You know, I swear I've heard this before. Where oh where have I heard this again? Oh yeah. You sound exactly like Bob. He came to me just as you are now. It is eerie---no matter how different you thought you two were in the end, you sound almost identical."

Bill stands up. "Fuck you, Steve. Don't act like you didn't benefit too from the removal of Bob. You didn't object to receiving two of his territories, did you? Who was the one who fought hard for that too, huh? Me! I did. You and I have the most influential territories in the nation. Or is that it, huh? Your family has never liked how many territories mine has controlled. That since the civil war, we bet on the north, and progress and when they won, we took control of the north-east. That over time has been the most influential territories held by any of the families?

Steve shakes his head and laughs. "Well maybe after you pass and we divide your areas up, that won't be the case anymore. Virginia, I think we all can agree, is more south." He winks at Bill.

Bill smirks. 'Well, as you say, Curt and I have a great relationship. Tiffany and Matthew remember and respect who fought for them."

"Tiffany is very formidable, and you are right, she has been a great addition, and I am sure she is very loyal. Matthew, though... over the last two plus decades, we have gotten close. Curt, although he is generally very liberal, is, let us say, a little less than politically correct when it comes to those of darker skin. And James... you played his anti-Latino bias perfectly. I am betting, though, that after I inform him of how Zach has all but disavowed his first wife and has a beautiful new fair-skinned wife from his hometown in South Dakota, I may be able to sway him to back a former member as your replacement. I plan to bring Zach back, then I can finally hold my head up high and fulfill my word to Bob."

Bill "Fuck you and Bob." Bill walks towards the door.

"Hey, no hard feelings, Bill. Listen, I'll keep an eye out for William. If one of the other families decides they want to cross me, maybe I'll bring him back into the fold. Now, on your way out, can you send that oh-so-fine dark skinned young thing back in here? I believe we have a lot more to discuss."

"You should know better than to count me out and think this is over Steve. Unlike Bob, I am not losing my mind. I have a lot of time left, and I will be making the most of it. You have a grand evening and enjoy."

Bill storms out, leaving the door open. Ray is waiting outside, talking to the concierge. He notices how quickly Bill is walking, indicates to the concierge that he will contact her later and quickly catches up with Bill.

Steve calls for the concierge, who goes into the office.

Bill and Ray enter the elevator. "Sir is there an issue?" asks Ray.

"Contact my son. I must speak to him first thing tomorrow."

Bill and Ray both exit the elevator and the building. "Hope you had a good evening, gentlemen." a new doorman says.

Ray opens the door for Bill and closes it after him. He acknowledges the new doorman before getting into the car and driving off.

CHAPTER 13

OLD LION VS YOUNG CUB

Chad opens the car door for William. He walks up towards his parents' front door. Bill opens the door and greets his son.

As they walk, "So how are things going son?" asks Bill.

"Things at the office are going well." William responds. "We are closing the merger on Wednesday. The plaintiff's lawyer, in the environmental case, funds are dwindling down. The government has failed to see any causation, so they have declined to pursue their claims, he just doesn't know it yet." William is smiling with a since of accomplishment as they walk through the house towards the deck.

"That's exceptionally good son, exceptionally good. Now how about that personal issue your mother and I spoke to you about?"

"Personal issue?"

Bill pops his son on his cheek. "You still think this is a joke. Sit the hell down!" William sits down while rubbing his cheek. You don't know how much we have been through for our family to get to this point. You are putting everything in jeopardy for a piece of ass?"

William stands up. "You not going to talk about Tineshia like that. If you could get pass your misogynistic and racist views..." Bill tries to hit William again mid-sentence, but he grabs his hand mid swing. "You would see just how strong and smart she is."

Bill snatches his arm away and sits down in the chair. "This cancer already making me slow, you know you wouldn't have caught me like that." William laughs. "I don't doubt you son, you have always been a far better judge of character than I have. If you say this woman is great, I believe you, but it still changes nothing."

"You have told me this group or whatever only accepts the best people. First off, why does me and her bother anyone? Yeah, her family may have some problems and yeah she may have a checkered past, but why not investigate who she is now?"

"Son she may be brilliant. She maybe someone The Organization would work with, but that is a far cry from letting her know the ins and outs. Call it misogamy, racism, or what have you, but The Organization is not bringing a black woman that close." Bill shrugs his shoulders. "It just is what it is son."

"There has to be other members who are not so closed minded. What about Uncle Steve? He has always been around like family, surely he could help convince some people."

Bill grabs William's arm. "Listen to me, you can't trust Steve do you hear me? Son, I really need you to understand how serious this is. The Organization knows you already have disclosed the existence of the organization to Tineshia."

"What do you mean?"

"Son please don't, ok? There is a video recording."

"What the fuck? So, you are saying are offices are bugged? What about attorney client privilege? We meet with clients in there. What about my right's? How did it get in there? Did you approve it?"

"Son, son. No, I did not approve it, but it was probably put in sometime within the last year. The only rules and rights we abide by are The Organizations. There is no recording, spying, or monitoring members unless the transfer of power has been started. Once my prognosis was confirmed to be terminal. I made it known I would focus my remaining time on getting you ready. So, you need to assume everything is being watched. There is nowhere and no one

The Organization can't get to if we need to. Our reach and resources are quite extensive." William looks at his father with disbelief. "Son if you genuinely care about this woman, you need to understand this. You told her about us, The Organization knows that an outsider, an unaffiliated person knows about us. You have now put her at risk. If she told her family, her friends you have put all of them at risk." William reaches for his phone frantically. "Don't worry son, she is safe. For now. A vote would have to be called for any action to be taken and a vote has not taken place yet."

William sighs in relief.

"But that does not mean one will not be called at a later time." William is in shock. "I am not an ass son or let us say I'm not just an ass. You are a grown man, and I am not trying to tell you who to love. I am telling you though, if you like your lifestyle, if you want to continue the legacy and traditions that our family has had for years. If you want to use your mind and combine it with our incredible resources to influence and effect significant change?" Bill stands up and puts his hand on William's shoulders. "If that is what you want son or even curious about. Then I am telling you there will be some sacrifices." Bill lightly pats William on his cheek, the same spot he popped him earlier, and walks away. William sits against the edge of the deck and twirls his phone. Bill yells from inside the house, "Will, meet me in my study before you leave, please."

Will continues to sit there and contemplates for a

few more minutes. He stands up and starts walking towards his father's study. As he enters, he sees his father sitting at his desk, with a set of files in front of him. "What, more dirt on Tineshia and her family?" asks Will.

"Please have a seat." Will sits down. "Being part of The Organization, is akin to making partner. Your connections and information are shared. What you know now becomes what The Organization knows." Bill slides the documents towards Will. "I suspect none of the families turn everything over though. Here are one or two that our family has kept to ourselves over the years."

Will looks at documents. "One or two? There are at least 10 folders here."

"Your grandfather told me for every two new contacts we make, we keep one for our own family and we inform The Organization of one."

"There seems to be very little trust going on for all the power and influence y'all claim to have."

"Many powerful people, with many different opinions, views, and styles. And they all are used to getting their way. It is prudent to have contacts that only you know of and can utilize at times to tip the scales if needed or....in the unlikely event you need protection. Anyone you bring to The Organization can be utilize by them at any moment for any situation. Whatever they are utilized for is put into a report, that is routinely reviewed."

William continues to thumb through the names on the sixteen folders. When he gets to one name, he becomes amazed as to who it is.

"I want you to take these home with you son. Perouse through them. Lock them away in your safe. They are incredibly detailed; lets you know how we initially got in with them. What their strengths and pressure points are. What their preferred method of payment are and things like that. I hope I have done well in conveying to you the gravity of things now. I am trusting you with our family's future."

William nods and stands up and starts to gather the folders. "There are more, aren't there?

Bill winks at his son and stands up, walks around the table and hugs William.

CHAPTER 14

NEW ERA?

A helicopter lands on Vail Mountain in Colorado outside of a remote cabin. Ray exits, followed by Bill and two additional members of his security team. After they clear, the helicopter takes off. At the cabin there is two big black SUVs, and three very warmly dressed armed security personal outside. Ray leads unarmed, followed by Bill, and the rest of his armed security team walk towards the cabin. Bill and Ray are met and frisked, then shown inside. They enter a two level fully furnished log cabin with a roaring fire. Matthew's head of security is standing arms crossed in front of a bookcase to the left of the living room area. Bill walks to the right of the large wooden table in the center of the room and sits at one end of the table. In front of the table is an oversized couch, with a bearskin rug laying on top of the hard wood floors, which is in front of the fireplace where Matthew is very animated on a phone call. Ray proceeds upstairs and checks the five bedrooms and two bathrooms. After clearing all the rooms, he comes down and stands in front of the wall behind

Bill, maintaining sight lines to the front door and door leading towards the kitchen.

"You have 48 hours, after that the distance between you and your competitors is going to start to shrink." Matthew says aggressively then hangs up the phone. He walks to the table with Bill. "Sorry about that Bill. These new money kids don't understand what it takes to last, you know?" Matthew starts to sit down and takes a deep breath. "How rude of me. Do you want a drink?"

"I'll take a Bourbon neat." says Bill

Matthew gestures toward his security, "2 Bourbons neat."

"I'll help with that." says Ray as he walks towards the bar.

"So, I can't say I was surprised to get your call, but I am surprised to get it so soon." Matthew says to Bill.

Ray pours the Bourbon for Bill, then takes a sip. Matthew's head of security looks at Ray and smirks, then pours Matthew's Bourbon.

Bill replies. "You and I have routinely seen eye to eye. I really didn't feel the need to make this call but didn't want to make it seem like you were being taken for granted or anything and I love it out here in the mountains."

Bill and Matthew receive their drinks. "Mm hmm,"

Matthew leans back in his chair and raises his glass as to toast and Bill does the same. "So, did you get some more news from the doctors? At the meeting you said you had a few years, right? Did something change?"

"No, nothing changed but you know me. I despise leaving anything to chance or waiting to the last moment."

Matthew takes another drink, and sits up in his chair, "ok then Bill, go head give me your pitch."

"Pitch? You really not going to make this easy, huh? I don't think a whole pitch would be needed but anyway...one of the most important, if not biggest crutch to The Organization is stability. No matter what is going on in the world, we come together, listen to reason and come up with a plan to help guide the United States and keep her the strongest country in the world. Over the many years, yes we have had a few significant problems within the families, but now is not the time for uncertainty."

Matthew takes another drink, "sounds a little like a pitch to me. So, at the end of the day, you are promising the status quo?" What if there are members who are looking forward to progression in The Organization.

"The question isn't if progression is needed in The Organization but when? Timing is everything. Progression at a time of instability could cause it to be polarized. Anyone who is more hesitant to change will exaggerate any and all momentary pitfalls. Which could slow or even setback progress."

"Un huh so, those who may be feeling that way...you are telling to what? Just be more patient? Wait until a new member, heavily influenced from the old guard, and impressionable takes one of the most powerful seats at the table and hope for the best?"

"Matt, we are talking about my son. I have time left, and there will be no stronger influence on him then myself. I also think my decisions and votes would make anyone with progressive thoughts feel as though they have someone of like mind in this "old guard." My decision years ago to get away from an 'old guard' in favor of a new voice and vision."

"It seems like it was just the other day. Yes Bill, you brought me in and I am forever grateful to you for that. Being able to be a real formative voice in how my country moves and is govern doesn't get lost on me. Everyday I wake up I am appreciative, and I have you to thank. But I also have noticed who has always been there over the few decades. At every family event, who is at your right hand? Steve. I believe your son calls him Uncle Steve. Bill takes a drink. "You see, you brought me in but after I was in it seems like you left me to figure things out for myself. So, it made me start to ask questions. James and Curt, instead of you Bill, toke me under their wing, these are the voices I had in my ear."

"Matt listen..."

"Bill, please let me finish." Bill takes another drink. "So, I ask them is it the way of The Organization to leave everyone to learn the ropes on their own? Why does it seem like Steve and Bill are keeping me at arms distance? Do you know what Curt told me? He told me not to take it personal. That probably Steve would never warm up to me because prior to my arrival there was infighting between Bob, Steve, and you. So bad he thought there was a chance, this whole thing may unravel. Curt told me that you and Steve were thick as thieves, but because you had a beef with Bob you did everything you could to hurt him as much as possible before he died."

"That is not the whole story Matt."

"He told me you found and pushed me through as a final fuck you to Bob."

Bill sits up in his chair, "Matt, I chose you because you were a bright young supreme court clerk. You were and are a quite talented in working a room and have a deep knowledge of our country's true history as well as strong ideas on how the country can continue to grow. Not to mention a hell of a good poker player with an uncanny ability to know when someone was bluffing. Yes, Bob and I had our problems, that is no secret. At the end of the day his mind was going, and what he was telling the world... let's just say there were many situations we all had to smooth over because he just didn't know what he was saying or doing anymore. So yes, I voted against his son. How could we value the impression he would leave? He was scorching the earth."

"I really would love to believe you Bill, I truly would. I wanted to dismiss what everyone was saying. That was until Tom died. Tom died and you came to me and others just as you are now and made a plea for Tiffany."

"Once again showing my desire and willingness to change and progression." Bill nods his head. "So how do you question my desire for progress."

Matthew finishes his drink and raises his glass for his security to refill. Matthew nods his head, "yes that is true, but then I noticed over the years how you have mentored Tiffany. You see it makes me think. Is big Bill a hypocrite? This the man I wanted to emulate and learn from, whom I wanted to one day call friend. Did he just use me to get revenge on a rival?" Bill shakes his head as he finishes his drink. "Or does the self-proclaimed progressive, actually think less of Tiffany? If so, does that mean he doesn't truly believe Tiffany was worthy, but fought for her because he was trying to piss on another one of our members? How could I believe someone who is just out trying to settle old scores can be truly considered a progressive?"

"Since my start in this I have always been a man of my word. I'm careful with what I say and mean exactly what I say. You were not a revenge pick, you were the smart and best choice, ok?" Matthew's head of security brings Matthew's drink. "The only effect the situation between Bob and I had on you being chosen, is that him losing his mind spilled onto his son. Now when it comes to Mrs. Bennett, I did stay closer to her than I did you but that was simply because she was the first woman. I fully believe every member should come in and find their own way, but Mrs. Bennett came into an all-boys club. I made myself more available to her because she broke thru a glass ceiling and wanted to make sure she felt support. It is no secret, not all members are happy that she is here." Matthew takes a sip of his drink. "One of the main reasons you were recruited was because I knew you didn't need your hand held and you have exceeded expectations."

Matthew's head of security walks up and whispers in his ear. Matthew stands up from the table, "Bill I hope this has not been too contentious of a discussion. As I said I will forever be grateful for how you fought for me."

Bill stands up, "no not at all. You had questions and I hope I laid to rest any doubts you may have had."

Matthew finishes his drink, "I know you said you didn't think you needed to make a plea and your right." As Matthew and Bill walk towards each other, "you said you have always been a man of your word." Matthew and Bill embrace each other. As they release their embrace, Bill grins. "So, I will take you at your word. You said you would rein in William about who he chooses to spend time with. So, I'm sure we will see this far before it is close to the end for you." Matthew turns and walks to his head of security, who is holding his coat. Bill's grin turns into much sterner look. Matthew as he is putting his arms in his coat, "but you know what is ironic? I been reading the files Steve provided on this Tineshia. She seems very smart and savvy. Her with William? Now that could be a real power couple. But I guess after you set the precedence with Bob's son and his wife, you just couldn't support that huh?" Matthew walks towards Bill, "but that would have really been a sign of progression." Matthew shrugs his shoulders and turns and walks toward the door, his head of security right behind him. "Have a great time while you are in-town, you know me casa su casa. If you need anything, don't hesitate." When Matthew reaches the door, he turns towards Bill with one hand on the doorknob, "you know you were right about something else too. I was a hell of a poker player. I would of love to sit at a table with you. Gentleman, have a great time. Matthew opens the door and exits.

Bill throws his glass against the wall. "*This motherfucker!* If it wasn't for me, this fucking guy would still be kissing some judge's ass in Colorado. He wants to talk to me progression." Bill scuffs. "I have to prove something to him? Who the fuck he think he is? Does he know who the fuck I am? Cause I ain't fucking hold his hand?"

"Fucking pussy." Ray says while shaking his head

"Nah, I hate that phrase. A pussy is way stronger than that weak ass weasel. Ray, please get me another drink, I'll clean this mess up."

"Sir, have a seat. I will do both."

"Fuck that, leave it for his maids or whoever to clean up. Pour yourself one too, have a drink with me." Bill sits down. "*Motherfucker.*"

As Matthew walks towards his car, he looks at his head of security. "You know the old man was right about one thing. I always was very good at being able to read tells, won a lot of money and favors at the poker tables. I know when someone was lying and bluffing. I was nothing to him but the final dagger in Bob's back. He comes here, to my fucking home, and acts as if I should be happy or something. Like a dog at his feet, grateful he threw me a scrap from his table. Damn prick! Talking about he didn't think he needed to make this call. Just showing respect my ass. He may have Tiffany in his pocket, but he going to find a rude awakening when he contacts Curt and James. Steve and Bill's old ways and beefs are in the past. We are the new wave."

"So you're not planning on helping his son?" asks his head of security

"I honestly don't care either way. He going to have an uphill battle at the end of the day. Steve ain't on his side and he is dangerous. To go against Steve, Bill going to need everyone on his side."

Security Guard opens the door for Matthew. "So, you want Bill out the way?"

"You not hearing me. I don't care about either one of these old fools. Their ways are over. They are smug old bastards, they may have been a part of starting all this, but their ways can't continue. The world is moving forward, and they will be left behind. If we want to keep our influence and position, we will have to leave them behind as well." His Security closes the car door. Matthew rolls down the window, "send the girls inside. Let the old man have some fun with what time he has left." Matthew rolls up the window. His Security walks to the other car and knocks on the window. Four women of different ethnicities come out. His Security walks them up to the front door and knocks.

Ray answers. "To help with the cold in case the fire goes out." states Matthew's head of security. He steps to the side and the girls walk in. "Have a good evening gentleman." He turns and walks away, and Ray closes the door.

Bill stands up from the table and takes a few steps towards the door. "What's going on Ray?"

In walks all four women in a line. "A gift from Matthew to keep warm." The women all have on arctic black winter coats and boots. Once Ray presents them and steps to the side, one by one they open their coats. Each is topless, revealing breast sizes from a full C to double D. All dressed in identical blue, red, green, and black lingerie on their lower halves to go with their thigh high boots.

Ray walks next to Bill, staring enthusiastically at the women. "Looks like your Matthew may not be as bad as we think.

Bill smirks, "Matthew has definitely been paying attention."

"Sir?"

"This was one of Tom's moves. He would never let a meeting leave on a bad note or word. Always leave your adversary feeling as though they may have reached you. The smug prick already knew before I said a word he wasn't going to help. The girls were already in the car. Their a fucking consolation prize." Bill grunts. "Okay Matthew. Okay." Bill laughs. "You want to play games, let's play." Bill starts to walk towards the steps leading upstairs. As Bill is walking, he stops and gestures to Ray. Ray walks up to him and Bill whispers in his ear. "Call for the chopper. Have them here tomorrow at 1500 (3 p.m.) hours. First thing tomorrow around 0900 hours have a car ready, quietly and under Matthew's radar. Make arrangements to buyout Rijo from 1000-1100 and Cherry from 12-1300 (1 p.m.) We will have some special guests." Bill starts to go up the steps.

"Chopper at 3. Car at 9. Private reservations at 10 and 12. Copy." Ray repeats.

"I'm going to get some rest, got work in the morning." says Bill.

From the bottom at the stairs, “but sir?” says Ray.

Bill stops halfway up the steps and turns around. “Yeah Ray.”

Ray points at the ladies still standing in a line. “The girls, sir.”

Bill looks down at the girls. “Oh, right. Well, I guess you going to be logging in some extra hours tonight. Don’t expect overtime pay.” Bill winks at Ray.

Ray smirks, “What about hazard pay?” Ray turns towards the ladies. “Ladies---who wants to join me for a drink?” The ladies walk with Ray towards the bar.

Bill looks down the stairs smiling and shakes his head. Bill continues up the stairs, then pauses at the top. Bill walks back and stares at one of the girls. Bill yells “RAY!”

Ray steps back from the bar so he can see Bill. “Yes, sir?”

“I think I will have another drink.”

“Yes sir, I bring it up right away.”

“You seem to be a little busy Ray. Why don’t you ask Ms. Emerald Green if she wouldn’t mind bringing it to me?”

Ray looks at the girls and notices the one in the green lingerie. He then looks back at Bill and smiles. "Absolutely, sir."

Bill continues into the master suite and sits on the bed and takes off shoes. Pulls out his phone and makes a call. "Hello, this is Mr. Johnson. I'm in town and we need to talk. Tomorrow morning 10:15 a.m. at Rioja. Bill hangs up, then places another call. While the line is ringing, the woman in the green lingerie walks in with two drinks in her hands.

"I heard you were thirsty."

Bill puts his finger over his lips and winks at her, while motioning to have her sit next to him. "Hello, this is Mr. Johnson. I'm in town and we need to talk. 3:00 P.M. at Cherry. Bill hangs up the phone.

She slowly walks towards Bill. "Mmm, you have good taste. Cherry is one of my favorite spots." She sits down next to Bill and hands him his drink.

"Obviously I have good taste, I did ask for you didn't I?" The Woman smiles. Bill takes a sip of his drink. "Now the question is how good is your taste?" Bill unzips his fly. The Woman takes a sip of her drink then puts it down on the floor. Places her hands on Bill's legs and gets down on her knees. Bill shoots the rest of his drink, as his head slowly starts to roll back.

CHAPTER 15

ALLOW ME TO RE-INTRODUCE MYSELF

It is 8:30 a.m. Ray is driving a 1991 red Chevy Caprice. He turns off the main road on to a dirt road that leads to the cabin. Ray walks up to the front door with two cups of coffee. As he opens the door, he notices Bill is downstairs sitting in front of the fire. "Good morning, sir. I wasn't sure you were up yet."

Bill stands up and walks towards Ray, "Oh yes I am up. This is a big morning. I haven't had to play these games in forever it seems like. I got to admit, I feel energized."

"I was just saying, after last night I thought you may have needed a little extra rest, sir." Ray smiles and hands Bill his coffee.

Bill smiles back as he takes the coffee from Ray. "Ms.

Green does deserves some credit for the spring in my step." Bill winks at Ray. "Did you pick up the files?"

"Yes sir, I also went by the safe house. Everything is in the car."

"Alright---let the games begin."

Ray grabs Bill coat and helps him put it on. Ray and Bill exit the cabin and get in the car. After a 45 min drive, Bill and Ray arrive at Rioja at 9:35 a.m. The owner of Rioja is standing outside of the restaurant. The restaurant has all the curtains drawn and looks closed.

Ray walks up to him, "Thank you for hospitality."

Rioja owner a middle-aged pudgy white man, wearing a red and black plaid shirt, blue jeans, and black boots. "I don't know about hospitality. You all have me out here waiting and do you know how many people I have had to turn away? How many of my regulars? I don't know how y'all do things in the big cities, but..."

As the owner is talking, Ray pulls out an envelope and hands it to the owner. The owner stops talking and opens the envelope containing $20k. "I hope this takes care of any inconvenience we may have caused.

Owner with a grin on his face and new attitude.

"Inconvenience? No inconvenience at all." The owner hands over the keys.

"Again, thank you. We will be done in a couple of hours." says Ray as he takes the keys and walks to the car.

As Ray returns back to the car, "That seemed to take a little long, any issues?" asks Bill

"No, just complaining about us costing him customers." responds Ray

Bill gets instantly upset. "W*hat!* We are costing him." Bill laughs. "Okay, I'll deal with him before we leave."

Ray starts the car up and drives around the back of the restaurant to the employee parking lot. Bill grabs the files. Ray gets out the car and opens the car door for Bill and they walk in the back door. Bill starts taking off his coat. He puts the files under his coat on top of the bar. "Ray, you mind whipping up some French toast? I'm starting to get a little peckish."

Ray goes into the kitchen, puts on an apron, and starts getting together ingredients to start cooking.

Bill sits down at the bar facing the back door and waits. After 5 minutes there is a knock on the back door. Ray puts down the batter he has been working on, wipes his hands off, and opens the door. In walks a white gentleman with his head down looking at the floor. Dressed in blue jeans, a brown hooded sweatshirt, and a black jacket with a black hat.

"Senator? Is that you? You trying to be incognito or something?" asks Bill. Gresten Smalls lifts his head. Bill stands up and walks towards him and embraces the senator, "It is you! You here in your urban camouflage." Bill laughs and smacks Gresten on his shoulder. "Didn't know who it was walking in here. Have a seat. How have things been? We haven't talked in ages." Bill and Gresten have a seat at the bar. "You want something to eat? Ray makes some mean French toast."

Ray, with the bag of bread in his hands, looks up awaiting Gresten's response.

"No Ray, thank you. I won't be here long." Bill and Ray look at each other, both raising their eyebrows. Gresten looks at his watch, "I'm here out of respect. My father, before he died, told me if I ever received a call from the Johnson's that I needed to answer and listen. So, I'm here. And I'm listening. But I don't see Matthew and Matthew is my contact in The Organization. So, I don't understand or know why I or you are here right now."

Bill and Ray lock eyes and laugh. Gresten stands up, "and that's our time. Have a good day gentleman."

"The lack of tact and fire of youth... Mmm. I bet that felt good to you, didn't it? Let me guess you don't like that The Organization calls, and you got to stop whatever you doing. You built yourself up from the ground up and don't feel like you must answer to anyone. You are a straight arrow. Uncompromisable, and blah blah blah." Bill mocks

"You are almost correct. Actually, I don't mind The Organization, but I am loyal. Matthew and I have a good mutually beneficial relationship. Since he is my contact for The Organization, but he is not here, this meeting seems in bad form or is maybe a test? Either way I don't like it or appreciate it. So, if there is nothing else, you gentleman enjoy your time here and if you want to speak to me again? Go through the proper channels and have Matthew reach out to me." Gresten starts to turn to walk away.

Bill slams his fist on the bar, "*Senator!* I highly suggest you sit your ass down. Who the hell you think you are talking to?" Gresten turns back around. Ray shakes his head but never stops cooking. "Proper channels? Boy, I am the Fucking Channel." Gresten sits back down. Bill takes a deep breath. "It's been a long time since I have been disrespected in such a manner, almost had me regress to my younger days. You senator are lucky I am more evolved these days."

"I meant no dis...." Gresten tries to say.

Bill cuts him off mid-sentence, "aht aht. No you have already said your peace. Don't demean yourself by trying to walk it back now. Now your father, he was a smart and pragmatic man. He knew better than to underestimate people.

Must of been a gene that skipped a generation. You don't realize just how privileged your sheltered ass is."

"I have never been..."

Bill cuts him off mid-sentence again. "Do not interrupt me again boy! There is a limit to how much disrespect I will take for a day, and you sir, have met your level. Now if I STAND UP... this talk will be over! So will your world as you know it. So, I strongly suggest you shut your mouth and listen. Now since you want to talk to me about my Organization, let me tell you about your family history."

Ray turns on the griddle and puts on the oil. Bill lifts his coat and reveals the files. Bill takes the first one off the top and opens it. "Now let's start with your grandmother."

Gresten "My grandma...?"

Bill looks up from the file. "Excuse me, please continue." Gresten apologies.

"Grandma to the Smalls dynasty. She died when you were 11 right? Well, I met her when she was 40 and boy was, she something to look at." Bill closes his eyes and starts daydreaming. "Your grandfather was a lucky man, but he didn't act like it. He was horrible to that woman." Ray starts dipping the toast in egg batter mixture and putting it on the griddle.

"Let me tell you a story. Now, I happened to be out here

on vacation. Not to long after we started The Organization. Now I was just a junior partner at my firm at this time and I was out here with the senior managing partner. Now he was a prick, colossal prick I tell you. He knew I was special but in order to make named partner he expected you to kiss the ring. So, he would take you on this vacation to Denver. I thought it was going well and I had it in the bag. So, we are leaving this bar, headed back to the hotel. I'm in the passenger seat and next thing I know I notice this guy rubbing on himself... I'm shocked, thinking in my head, he must really be drunk. He says to me.

"We been noticing your hard work, and you been bringing in great business to the firm."

Whole time he is still rubbing on himself. I'm trying to keep my eyes forward and not look. Thinking why must he talk to me while he playing with his cock. He must have some woman lined up at the hotel or something and he just can't wait. Next, he says to me.

"You think you ready to be a named partner."

"Eyes looking straight forward like I'm the one driving," 'yes sir. I would find that to be a great honor.'

Next, I hear that unmistakable sound women either love or hate to hear. The sound of a man's fly unzipping. He pulls out his pale little inch worm and puts his arm around my back.

‘Honored--- show me just how honored you are.’

I feel his arm trying to pull me. This man was literally expecting people to kiss the ring to move up. So, I’m a lawyer right? An excellent lawyer. I can talk myself out of anything. So, I start. Sir I’m not... He cuts me off.

‘I’ve heard it all before Johnson. You have your future in your hands right now, or let me say if you don’t put my Johnson in your hands, you won’t have a future. You not about to talk your way around this. Make your decision Johnson, how bad do you want it?’

He looks me dead in my face and takes his arm off my shoulder and slowly reaches for my hand.

I’m in total disbelief, trying to run through every calculation in my head. Everything seemingly moving in slow motion. Right then in the corner of my eye what do I see? A cars headlights heading head on for us. I reach for the seatbelt, that I don’t have on, nobody wore seatbelts at that time. As I’m pulling my seatbelt, he has a confused look on his face. He then looks up to the road and that confused look goes to frightened very quickly. I get my seatbelt clicked in, he is reaching for his seatbelt with one hand and tries to swerve to the right with the other. I guess the driver of the other car finally notices they are in the wrong lane, and they try to swerve back into theirs. But it is too late. *BAM!*

When I wake, I'm bleeding from my head, but luckily no other major issues. I look to my left and....this guy is pinned against the wheel. He never did get his seatbelt on. He is conscious and spitting up blood... I can never get that image out of my head. I open my door and fall out the car. I stagger to check on the other vehicle. When I look in the car, who do I see? Your grandmother and two of her friends. All with their seatbelts on. Now, again I'm a lawyer right? So, what the first thing I do? I pull out my disposable camera and start taking pictures of the scene. As I take pictures of your grandmother's car, I notice an empty pint of gin on the floor of the car. A truck pulls up, and I quickly put away my camera. A man jumps out the truck.

I passed earlier and went up to the gas station and called 911."

Bill looks at Ray. "Man...The days before cell phones."

Bill turns back to Gresten. "Now your grandmother door is jammed so it took both of us to pry it open. He had to use his knife to cut the seatbelt so we could pull her out. As we do, what do we see? Not one, but three pints of gin on the floor of the car. Ambulance pulls up and gets the other women out of the car. We go back to the rental to check on my boss, but he has passed.

Fast forward a bit. I'm laying in my hospital bed doped up on pain killers. I see the police walking around but nobody has come to take my statement yet. I'm wondering what is taking so long. Before the police come take my statement who comes into my room? Your father, who's the mayor at the time. He tells he already spoke to the good Samaritan, and was told how I helped get the driver out the car. Then revels to me that the driver is his mother. He says he knows I'm a lawyer from back east and asks what I remember.

I tell him I remember after I pulled his mother out the car I saw three empty pints of gin. I remember we were driving when a car came in our lane. We tried to swerve but there was nowhere for us to go. I remember the paramedics saying my boss was dead.

He tells me how your grandfather had just left your mother for another woman and her and her friends went out to help her deal with the pain.

I tell him, I'm sorry to hear that but they should have called a cab or something, not driving drunk. A man is dead!

He pulls up a chair and sits next to me. He tells me when the paramedics pulled my boss out the car, they noticed something strange. His penis was out. He asked did I have any idea why that maybe?

Of course, I deny.

He says a man has died and that is tragic, but it is nothing we can do to bring him back. He says that adding this to everything else his mom is dealing with would break her.

I ask what he wants from me? I mean, I'm sure the paramedics and the police saw the bottles same as me.

He says that he knows the officers on duty, the paramedics as well. The question is can we come to an agreement.

Now I'm in my mid 30's listening to this 26-year-old first time mayor talking about how he wants to come to an agreement. So, I start thinking about The Organization and we came to a mutually beneficial arrangement. My boss was blamed for drunk driving and my name was kept out of the report. I went back east, made named partner and eventually managing partner. Your grandmother made a full recovery minus a few scars. She was never arrested or charged. If what your father said was true she never drank again after that night. And your father helped us establish our foothold in the region, while we bank rolled his campaign's and helped get rid of his competitors. When you came of age and had an eye for politics he asked if we would extend our generosity to you."

"That's a great story and explain a lot actually." states Gresten. "But what it sounds like to me though, is that my dad under sold his position. What I'm hearing is that my grandma kept a dick out your mouth and that The Organization may never have made it out here without my families help. He should have demanded to be an equal, seems he was short sided and I am not my father. My father and grandmother are both dead. So, if you thought this would, air quotations, destroy my world you are sadly mistaken. If anything, this is just hearsay. Now, again, I don't know why you called this meeting, but this is outside the normal channels. What would happen if I called Matthew about this meeting? What would happen if The Organization heard of this backdoor shit? Unlike my father I will not pass on my opportunities. I see an opportunity when it's in front of me. If you want whatever it is you called this little meeting for and you want it to stay quiet? Then I think The Organization just got a new member. And you, you going to make sure I'm the one."

Bill smiles and shakes his head. Ray hands Bill a plate of French toast and juice and starts laughing. Ray takes off his apron and heads towards the door.

"I don't see what I said funny."

Bill starts eating.

"I want to know we have an agreement before we leave here today."

Bill looks at Ray, while chewing "I tried to warn him didn't I?"

"You can't save everyone, sir." Ray shrugs his shoulders

Gresten turns to look at Ray who is behind him by the door, then turns back to Bill. "Warn me? "I don't think you are in any position to be warning me right now."

Bill wipes his mouth and drinks some of the juice. "You are right about one thing...well, two actually. You are not your father, and you did not think." Bill opens back up the file. "Your father was more ambitious then you know, I think. There was a time he tried to over play his position as well. So, to your earlier comment, that if I was to try and go public with this it would just be hearsay?" Bill pulls out pictures from the folder and drops them on the counter. Gresten picks up the pictures and sees his grandmother passed out in the driver seat of the car and a pint of gin at her feet. The next picture shows three more pints on the floor of the car between the driver and passenger. The next picture shows damage to the car and two women passed out in the car. The last picture shows the damage to the other car and the dead man pinned to the wheel. "Hmm...you are up for re-election in 6 months right? Your platform is family values and the plagues of driving under the influence of alcohol and drugs right? Gresten is still flipping through the pictures. "Now that I think about it you were right about something else you said. If I thought this would destroy your world, I would be sadly mistaken." Bill grabs his coat and the other files off the counter. "You are a very gifted politician, possibly even better than your father. So, I'm sure, even with the addition of those pictures, you and your team could find a way to spin it and recover. You remember what I stated earlier? If I stand up this meeting would be over and your world as you knew it would be destroyed. You have three children correct? Two girls and a boy right, 18, 16, and 14 right? Your 16-year-old is a girl and got early admission to Harvard right?"

Gresten puts down the photos and a look of concern comes over his face.

"Relax, relax. Like her father she is uncompromisable. Great grades, steady boyfriend. I really think she is going to make you proud." Gresten's face eases.

"That baby boy of yours though." Bill stands up and opens the file and pulls out pictures. "14 a freshman and already cornered the drug market in high school." Bill places several pictures on the counter showing several hand to hands showing Gresten's son selling various drugs and pills. "I only have the one kid, but I have heard that second one is always a problem, but for you it's the eldest and youngest, huh? At least your oldest, she is discreet and working with a high-end escort service." Bill pulls out the flyers. Gresten drops the pictures of his son and looks at the flyers of his eldest daughter. "She is very beautiful and talented. Imagine my surprise when her and her fellow co-workers walked in my cabin last night."

Gresten drops the pictures and looks up at Bill with tears in his eyes. Ray slowly walks up behind Gresten. "You don't believe me?" Bill pulls out his phone and shows it to Gresten, "She is quite stunning in this emerald green little number."

"You son of a bitch." Gresten attempts to lunge at Bill but is held down in his seat by from behind by Ray.

"I told you, you had met your limit of disrespect. I don't take kindly to threats and strong-arm tactics. You think you can blackmail your way into The Organization. You pathetic little man. You can't even take care of your family. You running for re-election on family values?" Bill laughs. "Wait until they get a load of these. Going to be the quickest drop in Colorado history, but hey at least it will give you more time to work on your family." Bill walks past Gresten who has his head down and is still being held down in his chair by Ray, towards the door.

As Bill passes Ray, Ray releases his grip and pats Gresten on the back and heads to the door behind Bill. Gresten pop's up from his chair and quickly tries to go after Bill. Ray hears Gresten moving and turns around quickly and puts out his arms stopping Gresten.

"Bill, sir please. I am sorry. I truly am, please what can I do?"

Bill turns around with a stern look on his face, "I told you once I got up this meeting was over."

"Bill, sir, what would you do in my position? Don't punish me, my family for my ambition."

"First off what I would have done is listen before I speak. You don't flex until you know you the strongest cat in the room. Secondly, I wouldn't just run a campaign on family values but actually take care of my family. You have a solid wife and one of your three kids seem to be on the right track, but them other two going to be your downfall if you don't steer them right. Yeah, you are ambitious, but you have too many skeletons to go any further, let alone want to part of The Organization. Family is the crutch of The Organization, if your family can't be trusted, then you can't be trusted."

"I understand sir. I will get my affairs in order. I could use some guidance sir, Matthew only comes around when something is needed. Would you be willing to take on a mentee?"

Bill laughs, "Matthew...who you think brought us the escorts. You keep talking of Matthew as a partner. Why has he not brought this to your attention? I am old. I don't know if have the energy to be trying to teach anyone anymore."

"Sir, I would like to learn whatever I could. Fuck Matthew! I respect what y'all have built and I want to make a real imprint on this world and for my country."

Ray looks at Bill. Bill nods to Ray and ray moves from between the two of them. Bill takes a few steps towards Gresten. "You need to seriously humble yourself. I'm not sure if this is real. Are you realizing your position, or is this just an attempt to spin what was about to be the end of your career. Are you guided by your ambition or by your soul? Did your ambition keep you from seeing what was going on within your family? Are you going to try and fix things because I told you that is what is going to stop you from moving up? Or did you just have blinders on and now that you know you are driven to make it right?"

"Sir honestly...."

Bill cuts him off by waving his hand. "These are rhetorical, you can't answer or convince me, not now anyway. As you can see, I have eyes everywhere. So, I will see how things go and maybe just maybe you will see Ray again." Gresten looks at Ray. Ray smiles.

"See Ray again?" Gresten looks puzzled

"See, already, you need to learn how to be humble. The only reason you are meeting with me today is because of your father who you just dismissed as weak. He was a great man and someone I was glad to have known, but you son. You have not earned my respect. So, no you will not see me again until you do. If you see Ray again you should count yourself lucky. You want me to pay attention to you? Okay, be careful what you wish for. You have a lot of work to do to get your life in order and you don't have a lot of time."

"I understand sir. I will show you rather tell you what I can and will do."

Ray looks at Bill and points towards to his watch.

"Since we are talking about people needing to be humbled. Let's get to the reason for this meeting today. I need you to hold up and put a temporary stop on all Matthew's projects and plans in the area."

"Sir?" Gresten replies

"Is there a part of that that wasn't clear?" Bill asks

"No, I'm just confused. He is a member of The Organization. He hasn't always been present, but he has been at my campaigns and rallies."

Ray shakes his head.

"So I will chalk this up as you just not knowing, so I will give you a one-time pass. I do not like having to ever repeat myself. I have told you what I need you to do. I don't care what favors you have to call in, or what favors you have to give out. Either you will get it done discreetly or you can't, and I need to find someone else who can."

"Understood." Says Gresten.

"It is crucial that Matthew doesn't know what or why things are being held up. You won't be saved if he finds out it is you, and God help you if you try and convince him I had something to do with it."

"I get it." says Gresten.

Bill turns and walks towards the door, Ray and Gresten follow. As they walk outside the owner of the store is standing waiting.

“You gentleman finish? says the owner. “Would love to open back up for the lunch rush?” The owner rubs his hands together and is smiling. “Get a little money today you know?”

Bill stops and looks at the owner with disgust. “You don’t know who I am do you? You don’t know how many times your family business struggled and almost closed before you took over huh?” Bill turns and looks at Ray. “You see this is what happens when the older generation spoils the younger generation and doesn’t educate them on their history.”

“Excuse me? You are right I don’t know who you are, but I did you a courtesy. So, I think what you mean to say is thank you.”

Bill looks at Ray then back at the Owner. “Your dinner business accounts for 75% of your business. Why is that? Most of your return customers come for your happy hour specials and stay for dinner. 75% of your business is return customers or your regulars. That is down 10%. Why is that? Your biggest rival is that new spot that opened up a few blocks over a couple years ago. I forget their name. They have been getting the majority of the 15–24-year-old traffic. They also have cyphered away about 5% of your regulars each year due to their updated menu and generous portion size. You know the only reason why you are not losing more business to them? You have a liquor license, and they just can’t seem to get approved for one.”

“Just who are you and what you know about my business?”

Bill turns and looks at Gresten, "Do you know who this gentleman is?"

"Of course I know the senator. We had a rally for him?" states the owner.

"Senator I'm thinking of this place, what happens when a restaurants liquor license is under review?"

"I believe they are not allowed to serve alcohol until after the review is over." says Gresten

"Hold on a second, what are we talking about here?" says the owner.

Bill without acknowledging or looking in the owner's direction, "How long does a review take?"

"Depending on how backed up they are? I would say 3-6 months."

"I want the other guys, whatever their name is, we are no longer blocking their application. Matter of fact I want their liquor license approved by end of the month. Same time, Rioja here, I think their license needs to go under review for 3 months."

"Hold on there buddy, I don't know what is going on here..."

Bill interrupts the owner. “What is going on here is a lack of respect and I won’t stand for it. I don’t know you, but I do know the original owners of this here restaurant. I’m guessing you’re a son, nephew, idiot cousin or something, either way they called you last minute late last night and told you what you had to do today. Now for whatever reason you didn’t process that for that to happen something above your station was going on. Even when you saw the Senator here in a one-on-one meeting with me, you didn’t think to humble yourself and find out what was going on. You thought yourself on this level. You think I owe you a thank you?” Bill chuckles. “Boy, matter fact, give us that envelope back.”

“Excuse me?” says the owner.

Bill turns to Gresten, “make their review 4 months.”

The owner puts out both his hands, “hold on hold on.”

“If you don’t hand that envelope over in the next 30 seconds, we going to go to 6 months.” Bill starts counting down, “30, 29, 28, 27….”

As Bill is steadily counting down from 30, the owner trips and stumbles as he turns and runs towards his car.

“20, 19, 18….”

The Owner opens the car door, opens the glove compartment and retrieves the envelope.

"12, 11, 10..."

The Owner doesn't bother closing the car door and runs towards Bill to hand him the envelope.

"You still think you on my level? You don't hand things to me. You don't get to know my name. Who handed the envelope to you? 5,4..."

The Owner goes past Bill to Ray and hands him the envelope.

"1."

Ray takes the envelope and hands it to Bill. Bill takes the envelope and walks to Gresten. "At the end of the day I didn't get in this for the money, or even the power..." Bill hands the envelope of cash to Gresten. "What has always mattered most to me is *Respect!* Too many people think that their money or position means people should respect them." Bill turns and points at the Owner, "I respect a honest hardworking janitor more than this man over here that was handed this business because he was born into it." Bill turns back towards Gresten. "You were born into money, and politics, but what are YOU? Who are YOU? Are you someone I should respect? I'll be watching." Bill turns and walks to the car, and Ray pulls off.

The Owner walks to Gresten, "Now just who in the hell was that?"

"If they wanted you to know you would know." Gresten puts the envelope in his jacket pocket and walks towards his car.

CHAPTER 16

BEST MADE PLANS

Fe-Fe walks down a hallway with a briefcase in her hand, knocks on a door of a penthouse apartment. Shawn, Steve's 6'9 295lb driver, opens the door and lets her in. They both walk into the living room where Steve is sitting watching the news.

"Well, does the good doctor have my prescription?" asks Steve.

Fe-Fe hands Steve the briefcase. As he opens it.

"I was given specific instructions to keep this refrigerated until use." Fe-Fe states. "Also, that under absolutely no circumstances should someone currently undergoing treatment for cancer take this. It would be lethal if they are not treated with in two-three hours."

“Hmm, two-three hours you say?” Steve asks Fe-Fe

“Yes sir. two-three hours and after six hours it’s undetectable in their blood.”

“Awesome. So, we need to keep this on ice until we are ready. Then we need to make sure Bill is not found for at least six hours. Ideas Shawn?”

“That can be arranged sir.” replies Shawn

Steve hands Shawn the briefcase. “Go ahead, put this in the fridge until we are ready for it.”

Shawn walks into the kitchen.

“Any other word on our Johnson family?” Steve asks Fe-Fe

“I’m about to start back my surveillance of Tineshia.” Fe-Fe replies. I believe she will be Williams Achilles heel, he won’t leave her alone no matter what his father says.”

Steve laughs. “Bill shouldn’t be surprised. William is as hardheaded as his old man. We’re going to have to take care of this quickly though. William is quite charismatic and charming. Given enough time he will have the whole world loving this woman. Next thing you know, these wishy-washy members, going to turn The Organization in to some damn United Nations. We already have a woman as a member, but now a black woman? Next it will be a Sanchez, or Gomez, or Hernandez on the board. Why all they names end ez anyway?"

Fe-Fe shrugs her shoulder. Shawn walks back in the room.

"Alright. Back to business. Shawn, I need you to start scanning locations ASAP. We are not going to allow the Johnson's the ability to try and manipulate and talk their way out of this.

Felicia, get back on Tineshia. She has divulged our existence to one person already. Make sure she is not spreading our business to anyone we need to be concerned with.

I thought I would just have to get rid of Bill. Jr I thought we could just humble and bring back in the fold after I get rid of our Mrs. Tiffany Bennett. But William seems to be a chip off the old block. They both just might have to go if his jungle fever can't be cured. This my second run in with this Tineshia. She is strong and not easy to break. If she ends up knowing too much, we will handle the Wite family as well."

TO BE
CONTINUED
FALL 2022

www.ingramcontent.com/pod-product-compliance
Lightning Source LLC
La Vergne TN
LVHW020740300325
806995LV00002B/25

* 9 7 9 8 8 8 6 8 0 1 0 5 7 *